GATOR
CHAMPIONSHIP
Recipes

Presented by the
Florida Goal-Liners

Designed, Edited, and Manufactured by
Favorite Recipes® Press
an imprint of

FRP™

P.O. Box 305142
Nashville, Tennessee 37230
1-800-358-0560

Book design by David Malone

Library of Congress Number: 97-061428
ISBN: 0-9659341-0-1

Manufactured in the United States of America
First Printing: 1997
15,000 copies

Acknowledgements

The Florida Goal-Liners would like to acknowledge and thank the following for their help in the production of this cookbook:

Sara Brazda and Gator Boosters, Inc.
The Lady Gator Committee
University of Florida Alumni Association
University of Florida Athletic Association

Photography Credits

The Heisman Trophy and likeness of the actual trophy are registered service marks of the Downtown Athletic Club in New York.

Tim Black
Kathy Cafazzo
Ray Carson
Allen Cheuvront
Adrian Dennis
Annette Drowlette
Bruce Fine
Jeff Gage
Jay Metz
Herb Press
Jodi Stewart
C.W. Pack Sports
UF News and Public Affairs
UAA Sports Information Department

Contents

Introduction

The Florida Goal-Liners were born in 1979. The birth mothers were none other than Ward Pell, wife of Coach Charley Pell, and Monika Kirkpatrick, wife of Senator George Kirkpatrick. Ward Pell had traveled with Charley to visit with many Gator support groups all over the country. She found that there were many women who were as interested in Gator sports as the men. In Gainesville there were two organized men's clubs, the Quarterback Club and the Fightin' Gator Touchdown Club, but no club for ladies . . . so Ward and Monika, along with several other ladies, sent out letters to women in Alachua County and several of the surrounding counties. The response was overwhelming!

Now, over eighteen years later, the Florida Goal-Liners are still going strong! When we first began, we held football clinics to teach our club members everything they always wanted to know about football. Today, the coaches tell us we ask some of the hardest questions! Over the years we have enjoyed learning about all of our sports. The organization has over one hundred avid Gator women who enjoy meeting and discussing Gator events. We have participated in many projects: from buying computers, sponsoring the Senior Homecoming Float, working with the Cris Collingsworth Benefit, to contributing to an athletic scholarship endowment.

We are really excited about this latest endeavor. We have put together *Gator Championship Recipes* because we know Gators everywhere love to eat! These recipes have been collected from Goal-Liners, coaches and coaches' wives, former athletes, alumni, and Gator fans everywhere. We even have some recipes that we picked up from some of our rivals at away games. All proceeds from the sale of this cookbook will go to fund athletic scholarships.

We would like to thank all of our contributors who made this cookbook possible: the recipe contributors, the University of Florida Athletic Association, Gator Boosters, Inc., University of Florida Alumni Association, and all of the Florida Goal-Liners.

We would also like to dedicate this book in memory of one of our Charter Goal-Liner members, Vida Alexander. Vida was the wife of a retired military colonel and collected recipes from all over the world. She was an avid Gator fan until her death in 1995. You will see some of her favorite recipes throughout the book.

We hope you enjoy the cookbook! It's great to be a Florida Gator!

The Birth of a Nickname

Reprinted from *Florida Times-Union*, August 2, 1948
A Jacksonville lawyer christened the University of Florida's football team 41 years ago when he gave a pennant-designing firm in Charlottesville, Virginia, the suggestion of "The Alligators."

Austin Miller, who has practiced law here since shortly after his graduation from the University of Virginia in 1910, yesterday recalled the circumstances surrounding the choice of a name for Florida University's athletic teams. It happened in the fall of 1907, a year after the University of Gainesville had fielded its first team.

Miller, a native of Gainesville, was enrolled in the University of Virginia at the time and was visited by his father, Phillip Miller, a Gainesville merchant. The elder Miller, who died nine years ago, then owned and operated a combination drug store and stationery store in Gainesville, a popular rendezvous for university students.

While in Charlottesville the father decided to order some pennants and banners for the University of Florida from the Michie Company, which was engaged in the manufacture of such items. The Millers went to the firm, where they were shown samples of pennants which featured the Yale bulldog, the Princeton tiger and other school emblems. When the manager asked for Florida's emblem, the Millers realized the new school had none.

Austin Miller said the name "Alligators" occurred to him as a suitable emblem, both because the Michie manager said no other school had adopted it and because the alligator was native to this state. "I had no idea it would stick, or even be popular with the student body," Miller said. "We wanted to get the Michie firm started on the pennants as quickly as possible, though, so they would be available in time for the opening of the 1908 school term."

The Michie manager complicated the christening when he told young Miller he'd never seen an alligator and didn't believe he could design one. The law student volunteered to find a suitable picture of a 'gator. After much search, he said, he located a picture of one in the library of the University of Virginia.

The first appearance of the alligator emblem, Miller recalled, was in his father's Gainesville store in 1908. The Michie firm had supplied Millers' with the blue banner measuring six by three feet, showing a large orange alligator, and also with several different types of smaller banners and pennants. Some of them showed the alligator lying down, some rampant, while others included only the alligator's head.

Appetizers & Beverages

Gator Gatherings

Artichoke Dip

This recipe was contributed by Carl and Deborah Franks. Carl is assistant offensive coordinator and running backs coach for the Gators. He lettered at Duke at both running back and tight end and played professionally with the USFL's Tampa Bay Bandits under Coach Spurrier.

Pictured on page 9, the Gator Flag.

2 small jars artichoke hearts
1 cup grated Parmesan cheese
1 cup mayonnaise
6 to 7 drops of Tabasco sauce

Mash the artichokes with a fork and knife in a bowl. Add the cheese, mayonnaise and Tabasco sauce and mix well. Spoon into a glass pie plate. Bake at 350 degrees for 15 to 20 minutes or until bubbly. Serve with wheat crackers.

Yield: 15 to 20 servings

Black Bean Guacamole

$1/4$ small onion
1 (15-ounce) can black beans, rinsed, drained
2 tablespoons fresh lime juice
2 tablespoons fresh orange juice
2 cloves of garlic, pressed
$1/8$ teaspoon salt
$1/4$ teaspoon pepper

Chop the onion in a food processor fitted with a knife blade. Add the beans, lime juice, orange juice, garlic, salt and pepper. Pulse 3 times or until chopped, scraping the side of the food processor container each time. Serve with nachos or tortilla chips.

Yield: 20 to 30 servings

Swamp Dip

2 pounds ground beef
1 (28-ounce) can sloppy Joe sauce mix
1 can refried beans
1 cup spicy Bloody Mary mix
2 tablespoons Worcestershire sauce
1½ teaspoons chili powder
3 tablespoons chopped green onions
2 teaspoons celery flakes
Hot sauce to taste

Brown the ground beef in a skillet, stirring until crumbly; drain. Combine the ground beef, sloppy Joe mix, beans, Bloody Mary mix, Worcestershire sauce, chili powder, green onions, celery flakes and hot sauce in a large saucepan and mix well. Bring to a boil; reduce the heat. Simmer for 30 to 40 minutes or until thick enough for dipping. Serve hot with your favorite chips.

Yield: 30 to 40 servings

Gator Country Bean Dip

1½ pounds ground beef
1 large onion, chopped
1 small can sliced black olives
½ to 1 cup chopped green olives
2 small cans refried beans, or I large can
1 large jar mild picante sauce
2 cups (or more) shredded sharp Cheddar cheese

Brown the ground beef with the onion in a skillet, stirring frequently; drain well. Add the olives, beans and picante sauce. Pour into a shallow casserole. Top with the cheese. Heat in a 350-degree oven until the cheese melts. Garnish with chopped green onions.

Yield: 10 to 12 servings

Spicy Black-Eyed Pea Dip

1/2 green or red bell pepper, finely chopped
2 ribs celery, chopped
1 large onion, chopped
1 teaspoon pepper
1 1/2 teaspoons hot pepper sauce
1/2 cup catsup
1 teaspoon salt
3 chicken bouillon cubes
1/4 teaspoon nutmeg
1/2 teaspoon cinnamon
2 (15-ounce) cans black-eyed peas
1 (15-ounce) can tomatoes with green chiles
1 clove of garlic, pressed
1 teaspoon sugar
1/2 cup bacon drippings
3 tablespoons flour

Combine the bell pepper, celery, onion, pepper, hot pepper sauce, catsup, salt, bouillon cubes, nutmeg and cinnamon in a large saucepan. Cook over low heat until heated through. Add the peas, tomatoes, garlic and sugar. Simmer for 30 minutes. Add a mixture of the bacon drippings and flour. Simmer for 10 minutes. Adjust the seasonings and mix well. Serve warm with corn chips.

Yield: 30 to 40 servings

Bleu Cheese Ball

This recipe belonged to Vida Alexander, a Goal-Liner from 1979 until her death in 1995.

8 ounces cream cheese, softened
4 ounces bleu cheese, crumbled
1 (2-ounce) jar chopped black olives
1 teaspoon Worcestershire sauce
1 cup chopped pecans

Mix the cream cheese, bleu cheese, olives and Worcestershire sauce in a bowl. Shape into a ball and roll in the pecans.

Yield: 20 to 30 servings

Italian Cheese Spread

3 (8-ounce) packages Cheddar cheese cold pack spread, softened
11 ounces cream cheese, softened
1 envelope Italian salad dressing mix
$1/4$ cup dry red wine

Process the cheese spread, cream cheese, salad dressing mix and wine in a food processor until mixed. Serve with crackers.

Yield: 25 to 30 servings

Cheese Ball Dip

1 small jar dried beef
16 ounces cream cheese, softened
2 jars Old English cheese
1 tablespoon minced onion
Garlic powder to taste

Separate the beef slices. Soak in cold water to cover for 10 minutes to remove some of the salt. Arrange on paper towels to dry completely. Chop the beef into small pieces. Mix most of the beef, the cream cheese, Old English cheese, onion and garlic powder in a bowl. Spoon into a 4-cup serving bowl. Sprinkle with the remaining beef.

Yield: 20 to 30 servings

Mardi Gras Cheese Balls

16 ounces cream cheese, softened
1/4 cup finely chopped green bell pepper
2 tablespoons minced onion
1 teaspoon seasoned salt
1 (8-ounce) can crushed pineapple, drained
2 cups finely chopped pecans

Mix the cream cheese, green pepper, onion, seasoned salt and pineapple in a bowl. Add half the pecans and mix well. Shape into 2 equal balls. Roll in the remaining pecans. Chill until serving time. Serve with butter-flavored or other crackers.

Yield: 20 to 40 servings

Crab Spread

1 (10-ounce) can cream of mushroom soup
8 ounces cream cheese, softened
1 envelope unflavored gelatin
1/2 cup hot water
1/4 cup finely chopped onion
3/4 cup finely chopped celery
1/4 cup finely chopped green bell pepper
3/4 cup mayonnaise
12 ounces fresh crab meat, cooked

Heat the soup in a saucepan over low heat. Add the cream cheese, stirring until blended. Remove from the heat. Sprinkle the gelatin over the hot water and stir well. Add the gelatin, onion, celery, green pepper and mayonnaise to the cream cheese mixture and blend well. Stir in the crab meat. Pour into a mold. Chill, covered, for several hours to several days. Serve with crackers. For shrimp spread, substitute 1 pound cooked shrimp for the crab meat and tomato soup for the mushroom soup. For salmon spread, substitute 12 ounces salmon for the crab meat and 1/4 cup grated cucumber for the green pepper.

Yield: 30 to 40 servings

The Trawler's Famous Crab Dip

1¼ cups mayonnaise
1 teaspoon horseradish
1 cup crab meat
¼ cup French salad dressing
½ cup finely shredded Cheddar cheese

Mix the mayonnaise, horseradish, crab meat, salad dressing and cheese in a bowl. Chill until serving time. Serve with crackers.

Yield: 30 to 40 servings

Dill Dip

1 cup sour cream
1 cup mayonnaise
1½ teaspoons dillweed
1 teaspoon garlic powder

Combine the sour cream, mayonnaise, dillweed and garlic powder in a bowl and mix well. Chill until serving time. Serve with potato chips or crackers.

Yield: 25 to 30 servings

Homemade Mustard

1 cup chablis or other white wine
2 tablespoons dry mustard
2 tablespoons cornstarch
1/2 teaspoon turmeric
4 drops of Tabasco sauce, or to taste
1 to 2 tablespoons horseradish
1 cup cider vinegar
1 cup packed light brown sugar

Mix the wine, mustard, cornstarch, turmeric, Tabasco sauce and horseradish in a bowl and set aside. Bring the vinegar and brown sugar to a boil in a saucepan. Remove from the heat. Stir in the wine mixture. Cook until thick, stirring constantly. Remove from the heat and let cool. Pour into airtight containers. Chill until needed. Serve with ham, meat loaf or baked beans or as a dip for pretzels.

Yield: 40 to 50 servings

Chunky Salsa

1 (4-ounce) can chopped black olives, drained
1 (4-ounce) can chopped green chiles, drained
1 large tomato, chopped
1 bunch green onions, chopped
2/3 cup white balsamic vinegar
1/3 cup vegetable oil
1 tablespoon sugar
1/2 teaspoon garlic powder
1/2 teaspoon coarsely ground pepper

Combine the olives, green chiles, tomato and green onions in a medium bowl and mix well. Combine the vinegar, oil, sugar, garlic powder and pepper in a jar. Cover tightly and shake vigorously to mix. Pour over the vegetable mixture. Chill, covered, for 3 hours or longer. Drain before serving. Serve with tortilla chips.

Yield: 30 to 40 servings

Smoky Salmon Ball

   1 (15-ounce) can red salmon, drained, flaked
   8 ounces Neufchâtel cheese, softened
   1 tablespoon instant minced onion
   1 tablespoon lemon juice
   1 teaspoon prepared horseradish
   1/2 teaspoon Worcestershire sauce
   1/4 to 1/2 teaspoon liquid smoke, or to taste
   1/3 cup finely chopped celery

Combine the salmon, cheese, onion, lemon juice, horseradish, Worcestershire sauce and liquid smoke in a bowl and mix well. Shape into a ball. Chill for 2 hours or until firm. Roll the ball in the celery. Serve with crackers or fresh vegetables.

Yield: 30 to 40 servings

Joyce's Sausage Dip

   1 1/2 pounds bulk sausage
   8 ounces cream cheese, softened
   1 small can tomatoes with green chiles

Brown the sausage in a skillet, stirring until crumbly; drain well. Add the cream cheese and tomatoes and mix well. Serve with tortilla chips.

Yield: 40 to 50 servings

Gator Dip

2 pounds hot or mild bulk sausage
2 pounds Velveeta cheese, cut into chunks
1 (4-ounce) jar chopped pimentos, drained
1 (12-ounce) can evaporated milk

Brown the sausage in a skillet, stirring until crumbly; drain. Add the cheese, pimentos and evaporated milk, stirring until mixed. Serve warm with taco chips or corn chips.

Yield: 40 to 50 servings

Taco Dip

3 (16-ounce) cans refried beans with chiles
1 (4-ounce) can chopped black olives
1 (12-ounce) package guacamole
1 (20-ounce) jar salsa
3 cups sour cream
1 (8-ounce) package shredded 4-cheese blend of Mexican cheeses

Layer the beans, olives, guacamole, salsa, sour cream and cheese in a $2^1/_2$- to 3-quart dish. Serve with tortilla chips.

Yield: 20 to 25 servings

Marinated Cheese

8 ounces sharp Cheddar cheese
8 ounces cream cheese
$1/2$ cup olive oil
$1/2$ cup white wine vinegar
3 tablespoons chopped fresh parsley
3 tablespoons minced green onions
1 teaspoon sugar
$3/4$ teaspoon dried basil
$1/2$ teaspoon salt
$1/2$ teaspoon pepper
3 cloves of garlic, minced
1 (2-ounce) jar chopped pimentos, drained

Cut the cheese into pieces $1/4$-inch thick by 1-inch square. Arrange in an alternating pattern in an 8x8-inch pan. Combine the oil, vinegar, parsley, green onions, sugar, basil, salt, pepper, garlic and pimentos in a jar. Cover tightly and shake vigorously to mix. Pour over the cheese. Chill for 8 hours or longer. Remove to a serving platter. May serve with crackers.

Yield: 10 to 12 servings

Gator Tail Wings

1 (8-ounce) jar honey mustard
1 (18-ounce) jar barbecue sauce
$1/2$ teaspoon garlic
1 teaspoon lemon juice
5 pounds chicken wings

Mix the mustard, barbecue sauce, garlic and lemon juice in a saucepan. Heat thoroughly. Arrange the chicken in a 9x13-inch baking pan. Bake at 375 degrees for 40 minutes or until the chicken is cooked through, basting frequently with the sauce.

Yield: 10 servings

Baked Cream Cheese Appetizers

1 (4-ounce) can refrigerated crescent roll dough
1½ teaspoons minced fresh dillweed, or ½ teaspoon dried
8 ounces cream cheese
1 egg yolk, beaten

Unroll the dough on a lightly floured surface, pressing the seams together to form a 4x12-inch rectangle. Sprinkle the dillweed over the top of the cream cheese. Press the dillweed lightly into the cheese. Place the cream cheese dillweed side down in the center of the dough. Bring the sides of the dough up snugly around the cheese, pinching to seal. Place the cheese seam side down on a lightly greased baking sheet. Brush with the egg yolk. Bake at 350 degrees for 20 to 22 minutes or until light brown. Garnish with sprigs of fresh dillweed. Serve warm with crackers.

Yield: 16 servings

Tailgate Munchins

1 package granola with mixed fruit
1 package chopped dates
1 package fruit bits
1 package yogurt-covered raisins
1 jar dry roasted mixed nuts
1 package miniature chocolate chips
1 package butterscotch chips

Mix the granola, dates, fruit bits, raisins, mixed nuts, chocolate chips and butterscotch chips in a large zip-top plastic bag.

Yield: 50 to 75 servings

Tailgate Party Mix

1/4 cup butter
1 1/4 cups garlic salt
4 1/2 teaspoons Worcestershire sauce
8 cups mixed corn Chex, rice Chex and wheat Chex
1 cup pecan halves
1 cup pretzel sticks

Melt the butter in a large roasting pan. Stir in the garlic salt and Worcestershire sauce. Add the cereal, pecans and pretzels gradually, stirring until coated. Bake at 250 degrees for 1 hour, stirring every 15 minutes.

Yield: 50 to 75 servings

Baked Grapefruit

1 grapefruit
1 tablespoon sherry
Brown sugar

Cut the grapefruit into halves. Cut out the center; cut the membranes loose from the shell. Pour the sherry into the center. Fill the center with brown sugar. Sprinkle the entire top with brown sugar. Place on a baking sheet. Bake at 375 degrees for 15 minutes or until the grapefruit is very hot and the edges begin to brown.

Yield: 2 servings

Olive Balls

2 cups finely shredded sharp Cheddar cheese
1/2 cup butter, softened
1 cup sifted flour
1/4 teaspoon Tabasco sauce
1/2 teaspoon salt
1 teaspoon paprika
36 pimento-stuffed olives

Mix the cheese and butter in a bowl. Add the flour, Tabasco sauce, salt and paprika and mix well. Wrap approximately 1 teaspoon of the cheese mixture around each olive, covering the olive completely. Place on a baking sheet. Freeze until firm. Bake at 400 degrees for 15 minutes. Recipe may be doubled. May be prepared ahead and frozen unbaked.

Yield: 18 servings

Cajun Boiled Peanuts

1 (20-ounce) package raw peanuts
1/2 cup salt
1 package shrimp and crab boil
1 1/2 teaspoons ground red pepper
1 lemon, cut into halves

Fill a large saucepan 2/3 full with water. Bring to a boil. Add the peanuts, salt, shrimp boil, pepper and lemon. Reduce the heat but maintain a rolling boil. Cook, covered, for 4 hours, stirring occasionally. Remove to a slow cooker. Cook on High for 9 hours. Drain before serving. Serve hot or cold.

Yield: 15 to 20 servings

Spiced Pecans

1 tablespoon water
1 egg white, lightly beaten
3 cups pecan halves
$1/2$ cup sugar
$1/2$ teaspoon salt
$1/2$ teaspoon ground cloves
1 teaspoon ground cinnamon
$1/2$ teaspoon ground nutmeg

Beat the water and egg white in a bowl. Stir in the pecans, coating well. Mix the sugar, salt, cloves, cinnamon and nutmeg in a small bowl. Sprinkle over the pecans and mix well. Spread the pecans evenly on a lightly greased baking sheet. Bake at 300 degrees for 30 minutes, stirring occasionally.

Yield: 20 to 25 servings

Bacon and Sausage Roll-Ups

1 (12-ounce) package sliced bacon
1 package smoked cocktail wieners
$1/2$ cup (or more) packed brown sugar

Cut the bacon slices into thirds. Wrap each wiener with 1 piece of bacon. Place seam side down in a foil-lined 9x13-inch baking pan. Cover with the brown sugar. Bake at 350 degrees for 1 hour. Serve on wooden picks.

Yield: 8 servings

Bourbon Franks

1 (14-ounce) bottle catsup
1 cup packed brown sugar
1 cup bourbon
4 (8-ounce) packages miniature cocktail franks

Combine the catsup, brown sugar and bourbon in a saucepan. Simmer for 2 hours, stirring occasionally. Add the franks. Simmer for 5 minutes. Serve warm. May substitute two 16-ounce packages regular-size frankfurters cut into 1-inch pieces.

Yield: 30 to 40 servings

Gator Bait

This recipe belonged to Vida Alexander, a Goal-Liner from 1979 until her death in 1995.

1 pound ground beef or ground turkey
1 pound sausage or turkey sausage
1 pound Velveeta cheese, cut into cubes
Onion salt to taste
1 to 2 teaspoons Worcestershire sauce
1 loaf party rye

Brown the ground beef and sausage in a 400-degree skillet, stirring until crumbly; drain well. Add the cheese. Heat until the cheese melts, stirring frequently. Sprinkle with the onion salt and Worcestershire sauce. Spread on the bread to serve.

Yield: 40 servings

Wrapped Gator Bites

    1 package club crackers
    ½ slice bacon per cracker
    Grated Parmesan cheese to taste

Wrap each cracker with ½ slice bacon. Place in a baking pan. Sprinkle with cheese. Bake at 200 degrees for 2 hours. May be prepared ahead and frozen; reheat at 350 degrees for 10 to 15 minutes or until hot.

Yield: 8 to 10 servings

Some Like It Hot

    4 to 5 slices bacon, chopped
    2 cloves of garlic, chopped
    1 large onion, chopped
    3 pounds smoked sausage, cooked, cut into bite-size pieces
    4 cans baked beans
    3 tablespoons white vinegar
    5 tablespoons dark brown sugar
    ½ cup catsup
    2 teaspoons hot sauce
    1 teaspoon cumin
    1 teaspoon liquid smoke
    Cayenne to taste

Sauté the bacon, garlic and onion in a skillet. Combine the bacon mixture, sausage, baked beans, vinegar, brown sugar, catsup, hot sauce, cumin, liquid smoke and cayenne in a large Dutch oven. Simmer for 45 minutes.

Yield: 40 to 50 servings

Crab Bites

1 (7-ounce) jar Old English cheese
1/2 cup butter, softened
3 tablespoons mayonnaise
1/2 teaspoon garlic salt
1 teaspoon seasoned salt
1 (7-ounce) can crab meat, drained
6 English muffins, split into halves

Mix the cheese, butter, mayonnaise, garlic salt and seasoned salt in a bowl. Stir in the crab meat. Spread on the English muffins. Freeze for 20 minutes. Remove from the freezer and cut into quarters. Refreeze until firm. Store in freezer bags until needed. Arrange frozen bites in a single layer on a baking sheet. Broil until bubbly and brown.

Yield: 24 servings

Oyster Appetizers

1/2 cup butter
1 small onion, chopped
1 teaspoon minced garlic
1 1/2 cups freshly grated Parmesan cheese
1/2 cup bread crumbs
1 teaspoon hot sauce
1 pint oysters, rinsed, drained
1/2 cup sour cream
1 cup fresh spinach, lightly steamed, chopped
1/2 cup freshly grated Parmesan cheese
2 teaspoons bread crumbs

Melt the butter in a microwave-safe dish. Pour half the butter into a 10-inch quiche dish, coating the bottom of the dish; set aside. Combine the onion, garlic and remaining butter in the microwave-safe dish. Microwave on High for 3 minutes. Add 1 1/2 cups cheese, 1/2 cup bread crumbs and hot sauce and mix well. Spread the oysters in the quiche dish. Top with the sour cream. Spread the spinach over the sour cream. Top with the garlic mixture. Sprinkle with 1/2 cup cheese and 2 teaspoons bread crumbs. Bake at 450 degrees for 10 minutes. Serve with crackers.

Yield: 8 servings

Terry's Grilled Shrimp with Rémoulade Sauce

    2 pounds large shrimp
    1/2 cup red wine vinegar
    1/4 cup olive oil
    2 cloves of fresh garlic, sliced
    Rémoulade Sauce

Peel and devein the shrimp, leaving the tails on. Mix the vinegar, oil and garlic in a bowl. Add the shrimp. Marinate for 1 hour. Remove the shrimp from the marinade, discarding the remaining marinade. Grill the shrimp over medium heat for 3 to 5 minutes or until pink. Serve with the Rémoulade Sauce.

Yield: 6 servings

Rémoulade Sauce

    1 cup mayonnaise
    2 tablespoons chopped capers
    2 teaspoons Dijon mustard
    1/2 teaspoon parsley
    1/2 teaspoon chervil
    1/2 teaspoon tarragon

Combine the mayonnaise, capers, Dijon mustard, parsley, chervil and tarragon in a bowl and mix well.

Deviled Shrimp

    2 pounds shrimp, peeled, deveined
    1 lemon, thinly sliced
    1 red onion, thinly sliced
    1/2 cup pitted black olives
    2 tablespoons chopped pimento
    1/2 cup freshly squeezed lemon juice
    1/4 cup vegetable oil
    1 tablespoon wine vinegar
    1 clove of garlic, crushed
    1/2 bay leaf
    1 tablespoon dry mustard
    1/4 teaspoon cayenne
    1 teaspoon salt

Bring enough water to cover the shrimp to a boil in a saucepan. Add the shrimp. Cook for 3 minutes; drain immediately. Combine the shrimp, lemon slices, onion, olives and pimento in a large bowl and mix well. Mix the lemon juice, oil, vinegar, garlic, bay leaf, mustard, cayenne and salt in a medium bowl. Stir into the shrimp mixture. Chill, covered, overnight, stirring once or twice. To serve, spoon onto small plates or provide cocktail picks for spearing. Remove the bay leaf before serving.

Yield: 6 servings

Tortilla Roll-Ups

This recipe was contributed by Carol Stoops, wife of defensive coordinator Bob Stoops and mother of Mackenzie.

    16 ounces cream cheese, softened
    1 (4-ounce) can chopped green chiles
    1 (4-ounce) can chopped black olives
    1/2 teaspoon garlic powder
    1/2 teaspoon cumin
    10 flour tortillas

Combine the cream cheese, green chiles, olives, garlic powder and cumin in a bowl and mix well. Spread over the tortillas. Roll up and wrap in foil. Chill overnight. Cut into 1/2-inch pieces. Serve with picante sauce.

Yield: 30 to 40 servings

Spiced Cider

1 cup packed dark brown sugar
1 cinnamon stick
2 cups water
1½ quarts apple cider
4 cups orange juice
1 orange, sliced
Whole cloves

Combine the brown sugar, cinnamon stick, water, apple cider and orange juice in a saucepan. Bring to a boil. Top with orange slices studded with cloves. Simmer for 1 hour or longer.

Yield: 12 to 16 servings

Powerful Party Punch

4 quarts fresh lemon juice
2 (20-ounce) cans pineapple chunks
6 cups sugar
6 fifths of white wine
6 fifths of Champagne
3 cups orange curaçao
2 quarts frozen whole unsweetened strawberries

Combine the lemon juice, undrained pineapple and sugar in a large container and mix well. Add the white wine, Champagne, curaçao and strawberries just before serving time. Pour into a punch bowl. Add an ice ring filled with strawberries. Note: An easy way to prepare the ice ring is to fill a small tube pan with water. Stir in a few drops of red food coloring and some strawberry halves. Freeze for 24 hours. For a Christmas ice ring, use less food coloring and add some parsley sprigs.

Yield: 75 servings

Fruit Juice Punch

3 cups pineapple juice
2 cups water
2 cups apple juice
1 (6-ounce) can frozen lemonade concentrate
1 (6-ounce) can frozen orange juice concentrate
2 teaspoons lemon instant tea mix
2 cups chilled ginger ale

Combine the pineapple juice, water, apple juice, concentrates and tea mix in a large pitcher and mix well. Chill, covered, for 2 hours or longer. Stir in the ginger ale at serving time.

Yield: 15 to 25 servings

Swamp Water

½ gallon lime sherbet, softened
½ gallon ginger ale

Combine the sherbet and ginger ale in a large container and mix until smooth. Serve in a punch bowl.

Yield: 25 to 30 servings

Championship Punch

1 small jar maraschino cherries
3/4 cup lemon juice
1/2 cup plus 2 tablespoons brandy
1/4 cup plus 2 tablespoons curaçao
1/4 cup sugar
4 bottles Champagne, chilled
2 (32-ounce) bottles tonic water, chilled

Drain the cherries, reserving 1/3 cup juice. Combine the reserved cherry juice, lemon juice, brandy, curaçao and sugar in a large container and mix well. Pour over ice or an ice ring into a punch bowl. Add the Champagne and tonic water. Add the cherries if desired or reserve for another use.

Yield: 30 to 50 servings

Hot Buttered Rum

1/2 cup melted butter
1 pint whipping cream
1 (1-pound) package brown sugar
1 teaspoon ground cloves
1 teaspoon cinnamon
Boiling water
Rum
Nutmeg to taste
Cinnamon sticks

Let the butter cool to room temperature; any warmth will ruin the cream mixture. Combine the whipping cream, brown sugar, cloves and cinnamon in a bowl. Beat slowly by hand. Fold in the butter. To serve, place 1 heaping tablespoonful of the cream mixture in a cup. Add boiling water and 1 jigger of rum and mix gently. Sprinkle with nutmeg. Serve with a cinnamon stick. The cream mixture may be frozen and used as needed.

Yield: 30 to 40 servings

Orange Tea

6 cups double-strength sweet orange herb tea
2 cups orange juice
2 cups cranberry juice
Juice of 2 lemons

Combine the tea, orange juice, cranberry juice and lemon juice in a large pitcher and mix well. Chill thoroughly. Serve over ice.

Yield: 15 to 20 servings

Friendship Tea

1 cup instant tea
1 cup sugar
1 cup Tang
$1/2$ teaspoon ground cloves
1 teaspoon cinnamon
$1/2$ teaspoon nutmeg
2 scoops lemonade mix

Combine the tea powder, sugar, Tang, cloves, cinnamon, nutmeg and lemonade powder in a large container and mix well. Store in a tightly covered container. To serve, use 1 to 2 heaping teaspoons per cup. Fill with hot water and mix well. Serve hot or cold.

Yield: 75 to 100 servings

Hot Russian Tea

2 cups Tang
1 cup sugar
1/2 cup instant tea
1 (3-ounce) package lemonade mix
1/2 teaspoon ground cloves
1 teaspoon cinnamon

Combine the Tang, sugar, tea powder, lemonade mix, cloves and cinnamon in a bowl and mix well. Store in an airtight container. To serve, use 2 teaspoons per cup. Fill with hot water and mix well. Serve hot.

Yield: 75 servings

Whiskey Sour

Peel and juice of 12 lemons
4 cups whiskey
4 cups water
1 cup sugar

Combine the lemon peel, lemon juice, whiskey, water and sugar in a large container and mix well. Let stand for 24 hours, stirring frequently. Strain into a pitcher. Chill thoroughly.

Yield: 10 to 20 servings

Brunch

Warm-Ups

Artichoke Cheese Squares

2 (6-ounce) jars marinated artichoke hearts
1 small onion, finely chopped
4 eggs, beaten
6 saltines, crushed
8 ounces sharp Cheddar cheese, shredded

Drain the artichoke hearts, reserving 2 tablespoons of the marinade. Chop the artichoke hearts and set aside. Sauté the onion in the reserved marinade in a skillet; drain. Combine the onion, artichokes, eggs, cracker crumbs and cheese in a bowl, stirring after each ingredient is added. Pour into a greased 8x8-inch baking pan. Bake at 325 degrees for 35 to 40 minutes or until heated through. Let cool and cut into squares.

Yield: 8 to 10 servings

Chile Cheese Squares

2 (4-ounce) cans chopped green chiles
2 pounds Cheddar cheese, shredded
12 eggs
Paprika to taste

Drain the green chiles, reserving the liquid. Layer half the cheese, all the green chiles and the remaining cheese in a greased 9x13-inch baking pan. Beat the eggs with the reserved liquid in a bowl. Pour over the cheese. Bake at 350 degrees for 40 minutes or until a knife inserted near the center comes out clean. Sprinkle with paprika. Let cool and cut into squares. May cut recipe in half and bake in a 9x9-inch baking pan.

Yield: 20 servings

Pictured on page 35, George Edmondson, "Mr. Two Bits."

Bloody Mary Mix

3 cups water
1 cup tomato juice
1 (16-ounce) can tomato paste
2 tablespoons chopped canned green chiles, seeds removed
2 tablespoons dried onion flakes
2 tablespoons vinegar
2 tablespoons Worcestershire sauce
1 tablespoon lemon juice
1 teaspoon celery salt
1 teaspoon salt
1 teaspoon sugar
1/4 teaspoon garlic powder
Hot pepper sauce to taste
5 jiggers of vodka (optional)
Celery and/or carrot sticks

Combine the water, tomato juice, tomato paste, chiles, onion flakes, vinegar, Worcestershire sauce, lemon juice, celery salt, salt, sugar and garlic powder in a blender container. Blend until smooth. Season with hot pepper sauce. Pour into 5 glasses. Stir 1 jigger of vodka into each glass. Garnish with celery and/or carrot sticks to use as stirrers.

Yield: 5 servings

New Orleans Milk Punch

1 1/2 cups milk
1 1/2 cups half-and-half
1/2 cup plus 2 tablespoons crème de cacao
1/4 cup plus 2 tablespoons bourbon
2 tablespoons confectioners' sugar
2 egg whites
Nutmeg to taste

Combine the milk, half-and-half, crème de cacao, bourbon, confectioners' sugar and egg whites in a blender container. Process until frothy. Pour into glasses or cups. Sprinkle with nutmeg.

Yield: 4 to 6 servings

Cranberry Salad

2 cups cranberries
1¼ cups water
¼ teaspoon salt
1½ cups sugar
1 large package cherry gelatin
1 can crushed pineapple, drained
1 small can mandarin oranges, drained
½ cup chopped pecans or walnuts

Combine the cranberries, water and salt in a saucepan. Cook until tender. Add the sugar. Cook for 5 minutes. Pour over the gelatin in a bowl, stirring until dissolved. Chill until partially set. Stir in the pineapple, mandarin oranges and pecans. Pour into a mold or glass bowl. Chill until set.

Yield: 8 to 10 servings

Breakfast Bake

8 ounces mushrooms (optional)
1 pound bulk pork sausage
8 to 10 slices French bread, cubed
8 to 10 eggs, beaten
2 cups milk
1 teaspoon salt
¼ teaspoon white pepper
2 cups shredded sharp Cheddar cheese

Sauté the mushrooms in a nonstick skillet. Set aside. Brown the sausage in a skillet, stirring until crumbly; drain. Place in a 9x13-inch baking pan. Top with the bread. Mix the eggs, milk, salt, pepper and half the cheese in a bowl. Pour over the bread. Top with the mushrooms and remaining cheese. Chill, covered, overnight. Bake, covered, at 350 degrees for 45 minutes. May substitute bacon for the sausage.

Yield: 12 servings

Sausage Breakfast Casserole

  6 slices white bread
  $1/4$ cup butter or margarine, softened
  1 pound bulk pork sausage
  $11/2$ cups shredded mild longhorn cheese
  6 eggs, beaten
  2 cups half-and-half
  1 teaspoon salt

Trim the crusts from the bread. Spread the butter over the bread slices. Place in a greased 9x13-inch baking dish. Brown the sausage in a skillet, stirring until crumbly; drain. Spoon the sausage over the bread. Sprinkle the cheese over the sausage.

Combine the eggs, half-and-half and salt in a bowl and mix well. Pour over the cheese. Chill, covered, overnight. Let stand at room temperature for 15 minutes before baking.

Bake, uncovered, at 350 degrees for 45 minutes.

Yield: 4 to 6 servings

Spicy Egg Casserole

1 pound bulk sausage
6 eggs
1/2 cup flour
1 teaspoon baking powder
1 cup milk
3 ounces cream cheese, cut into small cubes
8 ounces small curd cottage cheese
10 ounces Monterey Jack cheese, shredded
6 ounces mild Cheddar cheese, shredded
1/8 teaspoon salt
1 bunch green onions, chopped
2 (6-ounce) cans sliced mushrooms, drained
6 tablespoons butter
Paprika to taste

Brown the sausage in a skillet, stirring until crumbly; drain. Beat the eggs with a wire whisk in a large bowl. Add the flour, baking powder and milk. Add the cream cheese, cottage cheese, Monterey Jack cheese, Cheddar cheese, sausage, salt, green onions and mushrooms and mix well.

Pour into a greased 9x13-inch baking dish. Dot with the butter. Sprinkle with paprika. Chill, covered, overnight. Let stand to bring to room temperature.

Bake at 350 degrees for 45 minutes.

Yield: 10 to 12 servings

Swamp Country Fare

1/4 cup butter or margarine
2 cups frozen hash brown potatoes
1/2 cup finely chopped onion
6 eggs, beaten
3/4 teaspoon salt
1/8 teaspoon pepper
2 tablespoons milk
3 tablespoons chopped parsley
1/2 cup shredded Muenster cheese
1 cup cubed ham
1/2 cup shredded Muenster cheese
1 tablespoon chopped parsley (optional)

Melt the butter in a skillet. Add the potatoes and onion. Cook, covered, over medium heat for 15 minutes or until tender and light brown, stirring occasionally. Beat the eggs, salt, pepper and milk in a bowl. Stir in 3 tablespoons parsley and 1/2 cup cheese.

Spray a deep 9-inch glass baking dish with nonstick cooking spray. Spread the potatoes and onion evenly in the dish. Pour the egg mixture over the potato mixture. Sprinkle with the ham.

Bake at 350 degrees for 20 minutes or until the eggs are set. Sprinkle with 1/2 cup cheese. Bake for 2 minutes longer or until the cheese melts. Sprinkle with 1 tablespoon parsley. Cut into wedges to serve.

Yield: 6 servings

Best Cheese Grits

This recipe was contributed by Martha Jane Green, widow of Bobby Joe Green, former Gator kicker and former UF volunteer coach.

3½ cups milk
1 cup grits
½ cup butter
1 (6-ounce) roll garlic cheese, sliced
2 eggs, beaten
½ cup milk
½ cup shredded Cheddar cheese

Bring 3½ cups milk to a boil in a medium saucepan. Stir in the grits gradually. Cook over medium heat for 10 minutes or until thick, stirring constantly. Remove from the heat. Add the butter and garlic cheese, stirring until melted. Stir in the eggs and ½ cup milk. Pour into a 2-quart casserole.

Bake at 375 degrees for 30 minutes. Sprinkle with the Cheddar cheese. Bake for 15 minutes longer.

Yield: 6 to 8 servings

Zippy Artichoke Oven Omelet

3/4 cup hot or medium salsa
1 cup chopped artichoke hearts
1/4 cup grated Parmesan cheese
1 cup shredded Monterey Jack cheese
1 cup shredded sharp Cheddar cheese
6 eggs
1 cup sour cream
Tomato wedges

Grease a 10-inch quiche dish or 3 small individual ramekins. Spread the salsa in the dish. Arrange the artichokes evenly over the salsa. Sprinkle with the Parmesan cheese, Monterey Jack cheese and Cheddar cheese.

Process the eggs in a blender until smooth. Add the sour cream and blend well. Pour over the cheeses.

Bake at 350 degrees for 30 to 40 minutes or until set.

Serve with tomato wedges. Garnish with parsley sprigs.

Yield: 6 servings

In 1993-1994 Florida accomplished a feat unmatched in intercollegiate athletic history. Never before has one school in one academic year accomplished all of the following: its men's basketball team advanced to the NCAA's Final Four, its women's volleyball team advanced to the NCAA's Final Four, its football team finished the year in the top five in the final Associated Press poll, its gymnastics team advanced to the Super Six, its women's basketball team was invited to the NCAA tournament, and its baseball team was invited to the NCAA tournament.

Cheese Soufflé

This recipe was contributed by Cheryl Doering, mother of Chris Doering.

> ¼ cup (about) butter, softened
> 7 to 8 slices bread
> 12 ounces Cheddar cheese, shredded
> 4 eggs
> 2 cups milk
> ½ teaspoon salt
> ½ teaspoon mustard

Spread the butter on the bread slices. Trim away the crusts; cut the bread into cubes. Layer the bread and cheese in a 1½- to 2-quart casserole. Beat the eggs in a bowl. Add the milk, salt and mustard and mix well. Pour over the cheese. Let stand for 1 hour.

Bake at 375 degrees for 1 hour.

This can stand overnight in the refrigerator before adding the egg mixture.

Yield: 8 servings

Chris Doering

Chris Doering, a second team All-America and a first team All-SEC choice in 1995, ended his career with 31 TD catches, the most in SEC and Florida history. A former walk-on who set a single season SEC and UF record with 17 TD catches in 1995, Chris finished his career with 149 career catches (fourth best at UF) for 2,107 yards (also fourth best at UF). He became just the 13th player in NCAA Division I-A history to catch 30 or more career TD passes and set an NCAA record in 1995 for most games catching at least one TD pass with 11. He was drafted by the Jacksonville Jaguars in 1996.

Crustless Artichoke Quiche

1 (14-ounce) can artichoke hearts
4 ounces fresh mushrooms, sliced
1 tablespoon melted reduced-calorie margarine
2 cups shredded Muenster cheese
4 eggs, beaten
1 cup skim milk
1/8 teaspoon pepper
1/4 teaspoon basil
1/4 to 1/2 teaspoon garlic powder
Paprika to taste

Drain and chop the artichoke hearts. Place on a paper towel; squeeze until most of the moisture is absorbed. Arrange in a 9-inch quiche dish sprayed with nonstick cooking spray.

Sauté the mushrooms in the margarine in a skillet until tender; drain. Pour over the artichokes. Sprinkle with the cheese. Combine the eggs, skim milk, pepper, basil and garlic powder in a bowl and mix well. Pour over the cheese. Sprinkle with paprika.

Bake at 350 degrees for 30 to 40 minutes or until a knife inserted near the center comes out clean.

Yield: 8 servings

Tomato Pie

1 can Hungry Jack biscuits (not buttermilk biscuits)
3 to 4 large tomatoes, peeled, sliced
1 tablespoon chopped fresh basil
Salt and pepper to taste
1/4 cup sliced green onions
1 cup mayonnaise
1 cup shredded Monterey Jack cheese

Line the bottom of a 10-inch pie plate with the biscuits (do not press biscuits up the side). Press the seams together.

Bake at 425 degrees for 5 minutes.

Cover the crust with tomato slices. Sprinkle with the basil, salt, pepper and green onions. Combine the mayonnaise and cheese in a bowl and mix well. Spread over the pie.

Bake at 425 degrees for 12 to 15 minutes or until the crust is light brown and the pie is cooked through. Let cool for 15 minutes before serving.

Yield: 6 to 8 servings

Spinach Phyllo

2 packages chopped spinach, cooked, drained
2 cups herb stuffing mix
1 onion, finely chopped
4 eggs, beaten
3/4 cup melted margarine
1/2 cup grated Parmesan cheese
1/2 teaspoon garlic salt
1/4 teaspoon pepper
1 package phyllo dough
1/2 cup melted margarine

Combine the spinach, stuffing mix, onion, eggs, 3/4 cup margarine, cheese, garlic salt and pepper in a bowl and mix well. Chill for 30 minutes.

Work quickly with 1 sheet of phyllo dough at a time, keeping the remaining dough covered with waxed paper topped by a damp towel.

Cut each sheet into 2-inch-wide strips. Brush 3 strips of the dough with a small portion of the remaining 1/2 cup margarine; continue to keep the remaining dough covered.

Place 1 tablespoonful of the spinach mixture on each strip. Fold over in triangle as you would for a flag. Repeat the process with the remaining phyllo, margarine and filling, keeping each triangle covered while you prepare the others. Place the triangles in a nonstick baking pan.

Bake at 350 degrees for 10 to 15 minutes or until golden brown.

Yield: 25 to 30 servings

Carrot Sandwiches

1½ cups shredded or grated carrots
8 ounces cream cheese, softened
Onion juice to taste
Salt and pepper to taste
1 cup finely chopped pecans
Mayonnaise
1 loaf bread, crusts trimmed

Mix the carrots, cream cheese, onion juice, salt, pepper and pecans in a bowl. Add enough mayonnaise to make of spreading consistency. Spread on the bread. Cut into finger sandwiches.

Yield: 20 servings

Italian Hero Sandwich

16 ounces Cheddar cheese, shredded
1 onion, chopped
1 (4-ounce) can chopped black olives
1 (4-ounce) jar chopped mushrooms, drained
½ cup vegetable oil
2 (8-ounce) cans tomato sauce
Oregano to taste
1 loaf Italian bread, cut into 12 slices

Combine the cheese, onion, olives, mushrooms, oil, tomato sauce and oregano in a bowl and mix well. Spread on the bread slices. Place on a baking sheet. Bake at 350 to 400 degrees just until bubbly.

Yield: 12 servings

Breakfast Rolls

This recipe was contributed by Mary Hafeman, who lettered in golf in 1978 and 1979 and won the 1980 Curtis Cup.

1 cup chopped pecans
2 loaves frozen bread dough, thawed
1/2 cup melted butter
1 (4-ounce) package vanilla pudding and pie filling mix (not instant)
1 tablespoon milk
1 tablespoon cinnamon
1 cup packed light brown sugar

Sprinkle the pecans into a greased 9x13-inch baking pan. Shape the dough into walnut-size balls. Arrange in a single layer in the pan.

Combine the butter, pudding mix, milk, cinnamon and brown sugar in a bowl and mix well. Pour over the dough. Let rise in the refrigerator overnight.

Bake at 350 degrees for 30 minutes.

Invert onto a foil-lined baking sheet to cool.

Yield: 12 servings

Breakfast Bread

This recipe was contributed by Kevin Thornton, head coach of UF Women's Swimming. He will serve on the U.S. coaching staff at the 1997 World University Games in Sicily.

9½ ounces water
3 cups bread machine bread flour
1 tablespoon dry skim milk powder
1½ teaspoons salt
2½ tablespoons margarine or butter
1¾ teaspoons dry yeast
3 tablespoons honey
3 tablespoons any flavor all-fruit jam
15 pecans, shelled, chopped

Combine the water, flour, dry milk, salt, margarine, yeast, honey, jam and pecans in the bread machine in the order listed.

Bake using the manufacturer's directions.

Yield: 1 (1½-pound) loaf

Three Florida swimmers have been named the Southeastern Conference Female Athlete-of-the-Year. Tracy Caulkins won the initial award in 1984, Dara Torres claimed the award in 1988, and Nicole Haislett (pictured here) earned the honor in 1993 and 1994, the first to win the award twice.

Nicole Haislett, 1993 and 1994 SEC Female Athlete of the Year and winner of four Olympic gold medals

Miracle Coffee Cake

18 frozen dinner rolls
1 (4-ounce) package any flavor instant pudding and pie filling mix
1/2 cup melted butter
2/3 cup packed brown sugar
1 1/2 teaspoons cinnamon
Chopped pecans to taste

Place the rolls in a greased bundt pan. Sprinkle the pudding mix over the rolls. Combine the butter, brown sugar and cinnamon in a bowl and mix well. Pour over the rolls. Sprinkle with the pecans. Let stand at room temperature, tightly covered with foil, overnight.

Bake at 350 degrees for 25 to 35 minutes or until golden brown. Let stand for 20 minutes before serving.

Yield: 8 servings

Soups & Salads

Cheesy Broccoli Soup

1/2 cup margarine
1 medium onion, chopped
4 cans chicken broth
2 broth cans water
1 large package frozen chopped broccoli
1 pound Velveeta cheese, cubed
2 cups half-and-half
1 package angel hair pasta
Garlic salt to taste

Melt the margarine in a large stockpot. Add the onion. Sauté until tender. Add the chicken broth and water. Add the broccoli. Combine the cheese and half-and-half in a microwave-safe dish. Microwave on Medium until the cheese melts. Stir to blend well. Add the cheese mixture and pasta to the stockpot. Season with garlic salt. Cook over low heat until the soup thickens. The pasta will disintegrate.

Yield: 15 to 20 servings

Corn Chowder

4 small potatoes, chopped
3 slices turkey bacon, chopped
1 (10-ounce) can cream of chicken soup
2 cans cream-style corn

Combine the potatoes with water to cover in a stockpot. Add the bacon. Cook over medium heat until the potatoes are tender. Add the soup and corn. Cook over low heat for 15 minutes.

Yield: 4 to 6 servings

Sausage Chowder

1½ pounds kielbasa sausage
1 large onion, finely chopped
½ cup chopped green bell pepper
1 (15-ounce) can tomato sauce
1 (8-ounce) can tomato sauce
1 teaspoon ground oregano
1 teaspoon chili powder
1 (15-ounce) can whole kernel corn
1 (15-ounce) can red kidney beans
2 tablespoons cornstarch
½ cup cold water

Slice the sausage into thin rounds; cut the rounds into halves if desired. Cook the sausage in a large saucepan just long enough to remove some of the fat; drain.

Add the onion and green pepper to the saucepan. Add the tomato sauce, oregano and chili powder. Add the corn and beans and mix well. Simmer over low heat for 45 minutes.

Dissolve the cornstarch in the cold water. Add to the soup gradually. Cook until thickened, stirring constantly.

May thicken the soup with 1 cup potato flakes instead of the cornstarch mixture. May add 1 cup water to the soup if thinner consistency is desired.

Serve with chili crackers or saltines.

Yield: 8 servings

Taco Soup

2 pounds ground beef
1 onion, chopped
2 cans stewed tomatoes
1 envelope taco seasoning mix
1 envelope ranch salad dressing mix
1 can pinto beans
1 can kidney beans
1 can yellow hominy
1 can green chiles
1 to 2 cups water

Brown the ground beef with the onion in a large stockpot, stirring frequently; drain. Add the tomatoes, taco seasoning mix and salad dressing mix and mix well. Simmer until heated through. Add the pinto beans, kidney beans, hominy, green chiles and water and mix well. Simmer until heated through. Serve with corn chips or crackers.

Yield: 8 to 12 servings

Venison Stew

1 1/2 to 2 pounds cubed venison
1/4 cup Kitchen Bouquet
1 small onion, chopped
1 can tomatoes with green chiles
1 bay leaf
Salt and pepper to taste
8 cups water
6 to 8 carrots, peeled, sliced
4 medium potatoes, peeled, chopped
1 cup dry red wine
Flour or cornstarch

Combine the venison, Kitchen Bouquet, onion, tomatoes, bay leaf, salt, pepper and water in a large heavy Dutch oven. Bring to a boil; reduce the heat. Simmer for 1 hour. Add the carrots and potatoes. Simmer for 30 minutes. Add the wine. Simmer for 30 minutes. Thicken with flour. May substitute beef for the venison.

Yield: 8 servings

Citrus Bleu Cheese Salad

2 pink grapefruit
1 envelope Italian salad dressing mix
$\frac{1}{2}$ cup vegetable oil
2 tablespoons water
10 cups mixed salad greens
2 oranges, peeled, seeded, separated into sections
4 ounces bleu cheese, crumbled

Peel and section the grapefruit over a bowl, reserving $\frac{1}{4}$ cup juice. Combine the reserved juice, salad dressing mix, oil and water in a jar. Cover tightly and shake vigorously to mix. Chill for 3 hours or longer. Layer the salad greens, grapefruit sections and orange sections $\frac{1}{2}$ at a time in a 4-quart bowl. Sprinkle with the cheese. Chill, covered, for 3 hours or longer. Pour the dressing over the salad just before serving time and toss gently. May substitute drained canned mandarin oranges for the oranges.

Yield: 6 servings

Congealed Salad

1 small package lime or other flavor gelatin
1 cup boiling water
1 can crushed pineapple, drained
1 cup whipped topping
1 cup cottage cheese
$\frac{1}{2}$ cup chopped pecans

Dissolve the gelatin in the boiling water in a bowl. Let cool. Add the pineapple, whipped topping, cottage cheese and pecans and mix well. Pour into a mold. Chill until set. Garnish with kiwifruit or lime slices.

Yield: 8 to 10 servings

Fluffy Pink Salad

1 (21-ounce) can cherry pie filling
1 (14-ounce) can sweetened condensed milk
1 (20-ounce) can crushed pineapple, drained
1 cup sour cream
12 ounces whipped topping
1 tablespoon lemon juice
1 cup chopped pecans or walnuts

Combine the pie filling, condensed milk, pineapple, sour cream, whipped topping and lemon juice in a bowl and mix well. Stir in the pecans. Chill for 1 hour.

Yield: 10 servings

Frozen Fruit Salad

This recipe was contributed by Jane Edmondson, wife of George Edmondson ("Mr. Two Bits," a Florida cheerleading fixture for 49 years).

1 teaspoon unflavored gelatin
1 tablespoon lemon juice
3 ounces cream cheese, softened
1/4 cup mayonnaise
1/8 teaspoon salt, or to taste
2/3 cup chilled whipping cream
1/2 cup sugar
1 (29-ounce) can fruit cocktail, drained
1/2 cup chopped pecans or walnuts
Lettuce leaves

Soften the gelatin in the lemon juice in a double boiler. Heat over hot water until the gelatin dissolves, stirring constantly. Blend the cream cheese, mayonnaise and salt in a bowl. Stir in the gelatin. Beat the whipping cream in a mixer bowl. Add the sugar gradually, beating constantly until soft peaks form. Blend the whipped cream into the cream cheese mixture. Add the fruit cocktail and pecans. Pour into a foil-lined mold. Freeze until firm. Unmold onto lettuce leaves. Let stand for several minutes to soften before cutting. May be prepared several days ahead.

Yield: 8 to 10 servings

Mixed Green Salad with Raspberry Vinaigrette

2 to 3 tablespoons butter
24 to 36 pecan halves
1 teaspoon (or more) salt
1 teaspoon (or more) pepper
Cayenne to taste
2 tablespoons sugar
Baby greens or European salad mix
1/2 to 1 pint fresh raspberries
Gorgonzola cheese or bleu cheese to taste
Raspberry Vinaigrette

Melt the butter in a skillet. Add the pecans, salt, pepper and cayenne. Add the sugar. Cook until the pecans are toasted, tossing to coat. Drain on foil, not on paper towels. Arrange the salad greens on a large platter. Add the raspberries and cheese. Toss with Raspberry Vinaigrette. Top with the pecans.

Yield: 6 servings

Raspberry Vinaigrette

2 tablespoons raspberry vinegar
1 tablespoon balsamic vinegar
1 shallot, chopped
Salt and pepper to taste
2/3 to 3/4 cup olive oil

Combine the raspberry vinegar, balsamic vinegar, shallot, salt and pepper in a small bowl. Add the olive oil and mix well.

Strawberry Pretzel Salad

This recipe was contributed by Carol Stoops, wife of defensive coordinator Bob Stoops and mother of Mackenzie.

2 cups crushed pretzels
³/₄ cup melted margarine
1 tablespoon sugar
2 (3-ounce) packages strawberry gelatin
2 cups boiling water
2 (10-ounce) packages frozen strawberries
8 ounces cream cheese, softened
1 cup sugar
12 ounces whipped topping

Mix the pretzels, margarine and 1 tablespoon sugar in a bowl. Press into a 9x13-inch baking pan. Bake at 400 degrees for 8 minutes. Mix the gelatin with the boiling water in a large bowl. Add the strawberries. Let stand for 10 minutes or until the strawberries are thawed. Mix the cream cheese and 1 cup sugar in a bowl. Blend in the whipped topping. Spread over the cooled crust. Top with the strawberry mixture. Chill until serving time.

Yield: 12 to 16 servings

Strawberry and Spinach Salad

Juice of 1 lemon
¹/₄ cup sugar
1 egg yolk, beaten
2 tablespoons vegetable oil
1 pound spinach
1 pint fresh strawberries, sliced

Combine the lemon juice, sugar, egg yolk and oil in a small bowl and mix well. Chill thoroughly. Wash and dry the spinach. Tear into bite-size pieces into a large bowl. Mix in the strawberries. Pour the dressing over the salad just before serving.

Yield: 6 servings

Artichoke Rice Salad

1 (8-ounce) package chicken-flavored vermicelli rice mix
1 (6-ounce) package fried rice mix with almonds
1/2 cup chopped green bell pepper
1/2 cup chopped green onions
1/2 cup chopped pimento-stuffed olives
2 (6-ounce) jars marinated artichoke hearts, drained, sliced
1/2 cup mayonnaise
1 teaspoon curry powder

Prepare the rice mixes using the package directions, omitting the margarine. Let cool. Combine the rice, green pepper, green onions, olives, artichoke hearts, mayonnaise and curry powder in a bowl, tossing lightly to mix. Chill until serving time.

Yield: 12 servings

Black Bean Salad

2 cans black beans, rinsed, drained
Kernels of 2 ears corn
1 clove of garlic, minced
1 medium onion, chopped, or equivalent amount of chopped
 green onions
1 green bell pepper, chopped, or 1 can chopped tomatoes, drained
1 small jar salsa
1 tablespoon olive oil
Minced fresh basil to taste
Chives to taste

Combine the beans, corn kernels, garlic, onion, green pepper, salsa, olive oil, basil and chives in a bowl and mix well. Chill until serving time. May add any other herbs of your choice. Serve alone or over pasta.

Yield: 5 to 6 servings

Linda Jowers' Broccoli Salad

This recipe was contributed by Ward Pell, wife of former head football coach Charley Pell.

Florets of 1 bunch broccoli, chopped
1 medium sweet onion, chopped
1 cup shredded sharp or extra-sharp Cheddar cheese
3 tablespoons red wine vinegar
1 cup mayonnaise
1/4 cup sugar
8 (or more) slices bacon, crisp-fried, crumbled

Rinse the broccoli and pat dry. Combine with the onion and cheese in a large bowl. Stir the vinegar into the mayonnaise. Add the sugar and mix well. Fold into the broccoli mixture. Chill until serving time. Add the bacon just before serving.

Yield: 10 servings

Ward Pell says that "Linda Jowers is not only a dear friend, but also the wife of Lieutenant Jowers, the State Trooper who travels with the Gators. Since the Jowerses have been friends for many years during and after our being at UF, we have shared holiday meals. Linda made a mistake by bringing this to one many years ago, and now it is a MUST when we potluck!"

Broccoli and Cauliflower Salad

This recipe was contributed by Jane Edmondson, wife of George Edmondson ("Mr. Two Bits," a Florida cheerleading fixture for 49 years).

1 bunch fresh broccoli
1 medium head cauliflower
1/2 cup golden raisins
8 slices bacon, crisp-fried, crumbled
1/2 cup sliced green onions
1 cup pecan pieces
2/3 cup shredded sharp Cheddar cheese
1 cup mayonnaise
6 to 8 tablespoons sugar
2 tablespoons vinegar

Break the broccoli and cauliflower into small florets and rinse well. Layer the broccoli, cauliflower, raisins, bacon, green onions, pecans and cheese in a large bowl. Mix the mayonnaise, sugar and vinegar in a small bowl. Pour over the salad. Chill overnight. Toss just before serving.

Yield: 6 to 8 servings

Walnut Chicken Salad

4 chicken breasts, grilled, cut into bite-size pieces
1 cup chopped walnuts
1 cup chopped green grapes
1 cup chopped red grapes
1/2 cup mayonnaise
1/2 cup vanilla yogurt
1 cup chopped celery
Salt and pepper to taste

Combine the chicken, walnuts, grapes, mayonnaise, yogurt and celery in a large bowl and mix well. Season with salt and pepper. Chill until serving time.

Yield: 8 to 10 servings

Tarragon Chicken Salad

4 boneless skinless chicken breasts, cooked, cut into chunks
3 to 4 ribs celery, chopped
2 tablespoons (heaping) sliced almonds
2 tablespoons dried tarragon
1 cup mayonnaise

Combine the chicken, celery, almonds, tarragon and mayonnaise in a large bowl and mix well. Chill until serving time. Serve over lettuce leaves or on sandwich rolls.

Yield: 8 to 10 servings

Victory Macaroni Salad

1 (16-ounce) package elbow macaroni
2 tablespoons olive oil
1 medium onion, chopped
1/2 large green bell pepper, chopped
3 ribs celery, chopped
2 (7- to 10-ounce) jars pimento-stuffed olives, sliced
10 ounces extra-sharp Cheddar cheese, cut into small pieces
2 teaspoons celery seeds
1/2 teaspoon salt
1/2 teaspoon pepper
1 1/2 cups mayonnaise

Cook the macaroni using the package directions and adding the olive oil to the boiling water. Drain and let cool. Combine the macaroni, onion, green pepper, celery, olives, cheese, celery seeds, salt and pepper in a large bowl and mix well. Add the mayonnaise and mix gently. Chill, covered, overnight. Garnish with additional celery seeds.

Yield: 6 to 8 servings

Lake Alice Ambrosia

4 ounces small pasta, such as shells, twists or wheels
1 (11-ounce) can mandarin oranges, drained
1 (8-ounce) can pineapple chunks
1 cup seedless green grape halves
1 small package lemon yogurt
1 tablespoon sugar
1 cup strawberry halves
1/2 cup shredded coconut

Cook the pasta using the package directions; drain. Rinse with cold water to cool. Place in a large bowl. Add the oranges, pineapple and grapes. Mix the yogurt and sugar in a small bowl. Pour over the pasta mixture and mix gently to coat. Chill for 2 hours. Add the strawberries just before serving. Top with the coconut. Best served very cold.

Yield: 10 servings

Vermicelli Salad

1 (12- or 16-ounce) package vermicelli
Salt to taste
1 teaspoon garlic salt
1 teaspoon pepper
1 teaspoon MSG
3 tablespoons lemon juice
3 tablespoons vegetable oil
1 small jar black olives, sliced
1 small jar chopped pimentos, drained
¾ cup chopped green bell pepper
1 cup chopped onion
1½ cups mayonnaise

Cook the vermicelli in boiling salted water in a saucepan using the package directions; drain and place in a large bowl. Mix the garlic salt, pepper, MSG, lemon juice and oil in a small bowl. Add to the vermicelli and mix well. Marinate in the refrigerator, covered, overnight. Mix the olives, pimentos, green pepper, onion and mayonnaise in a small bowl. Add to the vermicelli mixture and mix well. Marinate in the refrigerator, covered, overnight.

Yield: 8 servings

Marinated Pea Salad

½ cup vegetable oil
½ cup vinegar
1½ cups sugar
½ cup finely chopped celery
½ cup finely chopped onion
2 cans French-style green beans, drained
2 cans Shoe Peg white corn, drained
1 can very early peas, drained
1 can bean sprouts, drained
1 small jar chopped pimentos, drained

Combine the oil, vinegar, sugar, celery, onion, green beans, corn, peas, bean sprouts and pimentos in a large bowl and mix well. Marinate in the refrigerator, covered, overnight.

Yield: 8 servings

Red Potato Salad with Roasted Garlic Dressing

2¹/₂ pounds tiny red potatoes
2 green onions, minced
1 medium red bell pepper, chopped
¹/₄ cup minced parsley
Roasted Garlic Dressing

Boil the potatoes in water to cover in a saucepan until tender; drain and let cool. Cut the potatoes into quarters. Combine the potatoes, green onions, red pepper and parsley in a bowl. Add half the Roasted Garlic Dressing. Chill, covered, until 1 hour before serving. Stir in the remaining dressing. Serve at room temperature.

Yield: 6 to 8 servings

Roasted Garlic Dressing

6 cloves of garlic
3 tablespoons red wine vinegar
1 teaspoon Dijon mustard
³/₄ teaspoon dried thyme
¹/₄ teaspoon salt
¹/₄ teaspoon freshly ground pepper
¹/₃ cup olive oil

Roast the garlic at 300 degrees for 30 minutes in a garlic roaster or tightly wrapped in foil. Let cool. Cut away the tips of each clove; push the garlic from its peel. Combine the garlic, vinegar, Dijon mustard, thyme, salt and pepper in a food processor. Process until mixed. Add the oil gradually, processing constantly until thick and smooth. Pour into a jar or container. Cover and chill thoroughly.

Cold Rice Salad

This recipe was contributed by Judi Markell, head coach of UF gymnastics. She was the 1992 and 1994 NCAA Coach of the Year and has guided her teams to eighteen national championship appearances.

    8 ounces mushrooms, thinly sliced
    1 bunch green onions, chopped
    1 cup garlic salad dressing prepared from a mix
    1 package long-cooking wild rice
    Grated Parmesan cheese to taste

Combine the mushrooms, green onions and salad dressing in a large bowl and mix well. Marinate for 1^1/$_2$ hours. Prepare the rice using the package directions. Let cool. Stir the rice into the mushroom mixture. Sprinkle with cheese.

May use cheese garlic salad dressing and omit the cheese. Serve at room temperature.

Yield: 4 to 6 servings

Elfi Schlegel, Florida gymnastics

Tailgate Salad

4 (6-ounce) jars marinated artichoke hearts
4 packages chicken Rice-A-Roni
2 small packages fresh mushrooms, sliced
1/4 cup butter
1 tablespoon lemon juice
1 cup chopped mixed red, green and yellow bell peppers
1 cup chopped green onions
1 cup chopped celery
1 1/2 cups light mayonnaise
Lettuce leaves
2 small packages slivered almonds, toasted
Grilled chicken strips

Drain the artichoke hearts, reserving the liquid. Chop the artichoke hearts and set aside. Prepare the Rice-A-Roni using the package directions using 1 cup less water than the total given for all 4 packages. Sauté the mushrooms in the butter and lemon juice in a skillet. Combine the rice, artichoke hearts, bell peppers, green onions, celery and mushrooms in a large bowl and mix well. Mix the reserved liquid with the mayonnaise in a small bowl. Stir into the rice mixture. Arrange lettuce leaves on a serving tray. Place the rice mixture in the center. Sprinkle with the almonds. Arrange the chicken strips around the edge.

Yield: 16 to 20 servings

Seven-Layer Salad

1 (16-ounce) package frozen green peas
2 heads lettuce, rinsed, torn into bite-size pieces
1 red onion, sliced into rings
1 green bell pepper, sliced into rings
1 (32-ounce) jar mayonnaise
2 cups shredded Cheddar cheese
1 (3-ounce) jar bacon bits

Microwave the peas using the package directions. Alternate layers of the lettuce, onion, green pepper, peas, mayonnaise, cheese and bacon bits in a punch bowl until all the ingredients are used. Chill, covered, until serving time. May be prepared up to 3 days ahead and stored in the refrigerator.

Yield: 25 servings

Marinated Vegetable Salad

1 cup sugar
1 cup cider vinegar
1/2 cup salad oil
1/2 teaspoon salt
1/2 teaspoon paprika
1/8 teaspoon pepper
1 large can French-style green beans
1 large can peas, drained
1 (4-ounce) jar chopped pimentos, drained
1 medium onion, finely chopped
1 green bell pepper, finely chopped
1 cup finely chopped celery

Combine the sugar, vinegar, oil, salt, paprika and pepper in a small bowl and mix well. Combine the beans, peas, pimentos, onion, green pepper and celery in a large bowl. Add the salad oil mixture and mix well. Chill for 3 to 4 hours or until the flavors are blended.

Yield: 8 servings

Thousand Island Dressing

1½ cups mayonnaise
½ cup chili sauce
1 tablespoon grated onion
2 tablespoons finely chopped green bell pepper
2 tablespoons finely chopped celery
2 tablespoons finely chopped green olives
1 hard-cooked egg, finely chopped
2 tablespoons sweet pickle relish

Combine the mayonnaise, chili sauce, onion, green pepper, celery, olives, egg and relish in a blender container. Process until liquefied. Store in the refrigerator.

Yield: 6 to 8 servings

Poppy Seed Dressing

1 large onion, chopped
1½ cups vegetable oil
½ cup vinegar
2 teaspoons dry mustard
2 teaspoons salt
1 teaspoon poppy seeds
1 cup (scant) sugar

Combine the onion, oil, vinegar, mustard, salt, poppy seeds and sugar in a blender container. Process until liquefied. Store in the refrigerator.

Yield: 8 to 10 servings

Main Dishes

Game Time

Championship Hash

1½ pounds lean ground beef or ground turkey
1 large onion, chopped
2 green bell peppers, chopped
1 medium package yellow rice mix
1 large can chopped tomatoes, drained
1 cup shredded Monterey Jack or Cheddar cheese

Brown the ground beef in a large skillet, stirring until crumbly; drain. Add the onion and green peppers. Cook until the vegetables are tender.

Add the rice mix and the amount of water indicated on the package. Cook until the rice is tender and all the water is absorbed, stirring frequently. Add the tomatoes and mix well. Cook for 5 minutes.

Pour into an ovenproof serving dish. Top with the cheese. Heat until the cheese melts.

Yield: 6 to 8 servings

Pictured on page 73, "The Swamp," Ben Hill Griffin Stadium.

Monica's Quick-and-Easy Lasagna

This recipe was contributed by Monica Culpepper, wife of Brad Culpepper, a Gator All-America and a Tampa Bay Buc.

1½ pounds ground beef
Salt and pepper to taste
1 jar spaghetti sauce with meat
1 small package cottage cheese
1 package lasagna noodles
3 cups shredded mozzarella cheese

Combine the ground beef, salt and pepper in a skillet. Brown the ground beef, stirring until crumbly; drain. Add the spaghetti sauce. Bring to a boil. Simmer for 15 minutes. Drain any excess liquid from the cottage cheese.

Layer the lasagna noodles, ground beef mixture, cottage cheese and mozzarella cheese ½ at a time in a baking dish, ending with the mozzarella cheese.

Bake at 375 degrees for 40 to 45 minutes or until the noodles are soft.

Serve with garlic bread and spinach salad.

Yield: 10 servings

Frosted Meat Loaf

1 egg
1/3 cup quick-cooking rolled oats
1/3 cup barbecue sauce
1/2 teaspoon salt
1/8 teaspoon pepper, or to taste
1 1/2 pounds ground beef
1 (4-serving) package instant mashed potatoes
3 slices American cheese

Beat the egg with a fork in a bowl. Add the oats, barbecue sauce, salt and pepper and mix well. Add the ground beef and mix well. Shape into a loaf in a 4x8-inch loaf pan.

Bake at 350 degrees for 1 hour and 15 minutes. Remove from the oven and drain well.

Prepare mashed potatoes using the package directions, reducing the milk by half. Spread over the top and sides of the meat loaf.

Bake at 350 degrees for 15 minutes. Remove from the oven and top with the cheese.

Yield: **6 servings**

Jiffy Beef Stroganoff

1½ pounds lean ground beef
1 envelope onion soup mix
1 (16-ounce) package noodles
2½ cups (about) water
1 cup sour cream
1 can peas

Brown the ground beef in a large skillet, stirring until crumbly; drain. Add the soup mix and mix well. Cover with the noodles. Add enough water to moisten the noodles. Simmer, covered, until the noodles are tender. Stir in the sour cream and peas.

Yield: **4 servings**

Chris Couch, Florida golf

Marinated Flank Steak

This recipe was contributed by Cathryn Lombardi, First Lady of the University of Florida. Cathryn holds a botany degree and at one point was a cartographer. She has taught math and biology in Venezuela and is active in many community organizations.

Historian, teacher, administrator, and author, Dr. John Lombardi became the ninth president of the University of Florida in March 1990. He earned his bachelor's degree from Pomona College and his master's and doctoral degrees from Columbia University. He came to the University of Florida from Johns Hopkins University. A specialist in Latin American history, Lombardi is the author of seven books focused mostly on Venezuela. His wife, Cathryn Lee Lombardi, co-authored one of his books and illustrated two others. Dr. and Mrs. Lombardi have two children, John and Maryann.

2 tablespoons honey
1/4 cup soy sauce
2 tablespoons white vinegar
1/4 cup vegetable oil
1/2 teaspoon garlic powder
1/2 teaspoon ginger
1 1/2 to 2 pounds flank steak

Combine the honey, soy sauce, vinegar, oil, garlic powder and ginger in a large zip-top plastic bag. Add the steak. Marinate in the refrigerator overnight, turning once or twice.

Remove the steak from the marinade, discarding the remaining marinade. Grill the steak for 15 to 20 minutes or to desired degree of doneness. Slice cross grain to serve.

May double the amount of the marinade.

Yield: 6 to 8 servings

John and Cathryn Lombardi

Greek Rib-Eye Steaks

1¹/₂ teaspoons garlic powder
1¹/₂ teaspoons crushed dried basil
1¹/₂ teaspoons crushed dried oregano
¹/₂ teaspoon salt
¹/₈ teaspoon pepper
2 (1-inch-thick) rib-eye steaks
1 tablespoon olive oil
¹/₄ cup butter
1 tablespoon minced garlic
¹/₄ cup crumbled feta cheese

Combine the garlic powder, basil, oregano, salt and pepper in a bowl and mix well. Rub into both sides of the steaks.

Heat the oil in a large skillet over medium heat until hot. Add the steaks. Cook for 10 to 14 minutes or to desired degree of doneness, turning once. Melt the butter in a saucepan. Stir in the garlic.

Remove the steaks to serving plates. Pour the garlic butter over the steaks. Sprinkle with the cheese.

Yield: 2 to 4 servings

Rolled Steak Spaghetti

2 pounds very thin round steak, cut into 3-inch squares
1/2 teaspoon margarine per square
1/2 teaspoon parsley flakes per square
1/2 teaspoon bread crumbs per square
1/2 teaspoon grated Parmesan cheese per square
3 tablespoons vegetable oil
2 cans tomatoes
1 (10-ounce) can tomato soup
1 can mushrooms
1 can tomato paste
1 can tomato sauce
2 cloves of garlic, minced
Salt and pepper to taste
Hot cooked spaghetti

Place the steak squares on a sheet of waxed paper. Spread with the margarine. Sprinkle the steak with parsley flakes, bread crumbs and cheese. Roll up as for a jelly roll and tie with kitchen string.

Brown the steak in the oil in a large skillet. Add a mixture of the tomatoes, soup, mushrooms, tomato paste, tomato sauce, garlic, salt and pepper. Cook over low heat or in a slow cooker for 2 to 3 hours or until the steak is very tender. Remove the string from the steak.

Serve the steak and sauce over the spaghetti.

Yield: 6 servings

Steve Spurrier's Favorite Beef Barbecue Sandwiches

This recipe was contributed by Jerri Spurrier, wife of head football coach Steve Spurrier and mother of Steve, Jr., Lisa, Amy, and Scotty. A native of Ft. Lauderdale, she is a 1967 UF alumna. She is very active in the community and teaches aerobics.

    3 ounces liquid smoke
    Minced garlic to taste
    Pepper to taste
    Onion salt or garlic salt to taste
    Meat tenderizer
    Worcestershire sauce to taste
    1 (6-pound) boneless sirloin steak

Combine the liquid smoke, garlic, pepper, onion salt, meat tenderizer and Worcestershire sauce in a large container. Add the steak. Marinate in the refrigerator for 24 to 48 hours. Remove the steak to a roasting pan. Pour the remaining marinade over the steak. Bake, covered, at 275 degrees for 5 hours. Let cool in the refrigerator. Slice just before serving to avoid dryness. Serve on sandwich rolls with horseradish, lettuce, tomato and mayonnaise or with the Barbecue Sauce below.

Yield: 8 to 12 servings

Barbecue Sauce

    1 (14-ounce) bottle catsup
    1 (12-ounce) bottle chili sauce
    1/2 teaspoon prepared mustard
    1 1/2 cups packed brown sugar
    2 tablespoons pepper
    1 1/2 cups wine vinegar
    1 cup lemon juice
    1/2 cup thick steak sauce
    Tabasco sauce to taste
    1/4 tablespoon soy sauce
    2 tablespoons vegetable oil
    1 can beer
    Minced garlic to taste

Combine the catsup, chili sauce, mustard, brown sugar, pepper, vinegar, lemon juice, steak sauce, Tabasco sauce, soy sauce, oil, beer and garlic in a large bowl and mix well. Pour into six 1-pint jars. Store in the refrigerator or freezer.

Roast Beef Burgers

This recipe was contributed by Wanda Aldy, wife of Ron Aldy, former women's associate basketball coach.

1 onion, finely chopped
1 (8-ounce) can tomato sauce
1 tomato sauce can water
3 tablespoons Worcestershire sauce
1 tablespoon hot sauce
1 (12-ounce) can roast beef, chopped
1/2 bottle catsup
Salt to taste
Toasted hamburger buns

Place the onion in a greased skillet. Add the tomato sauce, water, Worcestershire sauce and hot sauce. Add the beef and catsup. Season with salt. Cook slowly until the liquid is somewhat reduced. Serve over the buns.

May substitute steamed or oven-roasted roast beef for canned roast beef.

Yield: 4 to 6 servings

Swamp-Style Prime Rib

1/2 cup grainy mustard
2 tablespoons honey
2 tablespoons chopped parsley
1 teaspoon grated orange peel
1/2 teaspoon salt
1/4 teaspoon pepper
1 (7-pound) standing rib roast
3 tablespoons flour
1 cup water

Preheat the oven to 425 degrees.

Combine the mustard, honey, parsley, orange peel, salt and pepper in a bowl and mix well. Spread over the roast. Place the roast meat side up on a rack in a roasting pan. Reduce the oven temperature to 350 degrees.

Roast for 2¹/2 hours or until a meat thermometer registers 130 degrees for medium-rare. Let stand, covered, for 15 minutes before carving.

Skim any fat from the roasting pan. Place the pan over 2 stove burners at medium heat. Whisk in a mixture of the flour and water, stirring to scrape up any brown bits. Bring to a boil.

Cook for 5 minutes or until thickened. Serve on the side with the prime rib and seasonal vegetables.

Yield: **8 servings**

Sauerbraten

1 (4- to 5-pound) rump or brisket pot roast
3/4 cup water
1 1/2 cups malt vinegar
1 tablespoon salt
6 tablespoons brown sugar
1/2 teaspoon ground cloves
1/2 teaspoon ground allspice
2 teaspoons MSG
2 teaspoons ground ginger
2 bay leaves
2 teaspoons coarsely ground pepper
1 cup chopped onions
3/4 cup water
Flour

Brown the roast in a heavy Dutch oven; drain. Return the roast to the Dutch oven. Add 3/4 cup water. Simmer, covered, for 1 hour.

Remove the roast and slice in half. Cut each half into 1/2-inch slices. Return to the Dutch oven.

Bring the vinegar, salt, brown sugar, cloves, allspice, MSG, ginger, bay leaves, pepper, onions and 3/4 cup water to a boil in a saucepan. Pour over the roast. Simmer for 2 to 3 hours or until the meat almost falls apart. Remove the roast to a serving plate.

Strain the cooking liquid and return to the Dutch oven. Add a mixture of flour and a small amount of cold water. Simmer for several minutes, stirring frequently. Pour over the roast.

Serve with mashed potatoes and red cabbage.

Yield: 6 to 8 servings

Chicken Noodle Casserole

3 whole chicken breasts, split into halves
1 cup chopped onions
1 cup chopped green bell pepper
1 cup chopped celery
8 ounces Velveeta cheese, cubed
1 (10-ounce) can cream of mushroom soup
1 (4-ounce) can mushrooms, drained
2 (5-ounce) packages noodles
1 cup cheese cracker crumbs
1/4 cup butter

Rinse the chicken. Cook in water to cover in a large saucepan until tender; drain, reserving the stock. Chop the chicken into bite-size pieces, discarding the skin and bones.

Sauté the onions, green pepper and celery in a nonstick skillet. Add the cheese. Cook until the cheese melts. Add the soup and mushrooms and mix well. Add the chicken and noodles and mix gently.

Pour into a greased 9x13-inch baking pan. Pour the reserved stock over the casserole. Sprinkle with the cracker crumbs. Dot with the butter.

Bake at 325 degrees for 40 to 45 minutes or until heated through.

Yield: 6 to 8 servings

Chicken Parmesan

This recipe was contributed by Missy Aggert, who finished her Lady Gator volleyball career ranked second on Florida's all-time career assists list. Missy was a first team GTE/CoSIDA Academic All-America for both her junior and senior years.

3/4 cup dry bread crumbs
1/2 cup grated Parmesan cheese
1 tablespoon vegetable oil
4 boneless chicken breasts
1/2 cup (about) flour
2 eggs, beaten
2 tablespoons butter
1 1/4 cups milk
1 teaspoon salt
1/4 teaspoon pepper
1/4 teaspoon dried basil
1/4 teaspoon dried oregano
3/4 cup spaghetti sauce
1 cup shredded mozzarella cheese

Mix the bread crumbs and 1/4 cup of the Parmesan cheese in a bowl and set aside. Line a baking dish with foil. Brush the foil with the oil.

Rinse the chicken and pat dry. Flatten the chicken slightly. Dust lightly with some of the flour; dip into the eggs. Coat with the bread crumb mixture. Arrange the chicken in a single layer in the baking dish.

Bake at 400 degrees for 20 minutes.

Melt the butter in a saucepan. Whisk in 2 tablespoons of the flour. Cook for 3 minutes or until brown, stirring frequently. Whisk in the milk and bring to a gentle boil. Add the salt, pepper, basil and oregano. Reduce the heat. Cook for 5 minutes, stirring frequently.

Spread the butter sauce over each chicken piece. Drizzle with the spaghetti sauce. Sprinkle with the mozzarella cheese and the remaining 1/4 cup Parmesan cheese. Bake for 15 to 20 minutes or until the chicken is cooked through.

Serve as a separate entrée or over your choice of pasta.

Yield: 4 servings

Norm's Chicken Salsa

This recipe was contributed by associate athletic director Norm Carlson. A UF graduate, he is the Sports Information Department's historian and a longtime assistant to Coach Spurrier.

    4 boneless skinless chicken breasts
    3 tablespoons salsa

Rinse the chicken and pat dry. Place on a foil square. Fold the smaller end of the chicken under for uniform cooking. Spoon the salsa over the chicken. Fold the edges of the foil to seal. Bake at 375 degrees for 35 minutes or until the chicken is cooked through.

Yield: 4 servings

Chicken Sherry

    4 large boneless skinless chicken breasts
    Flour
    Salt and pepper to taste
    1/2 cup melted butter
    6 to 10 ounces dry sherry
    1 (4-ounce) can sliced mushrooms

Rinse the chicken and pat dry. Flour the chicken and season with salt and pepper. Place the chicken in a baking dish. Pour the butter over the chicken. Bake at 350 degrees for 30 minutes. Reduce the oven temperature to 325 degrees. Add the sherry and mushrooms. Bake for 30 minutes or until the chicken is cooked through.

Yield: 4 servings

Chicken Tortilla Casserole

This recipe was contributed by Carol Stoops, wife of defensive coordinator Bob Stoops and mother of Mackenzie.

6 whole chicken breasts
2 ribs celery, chopped
1 onion, chopped
1 (10-ounce) can cream of chicken soup
1 (10-ounce) can cream of mushroom soup
1 cup milk
1 small onion, grated
2 cans green chile salsa
1 can chicken broth
12 corn tortillas, cut into 1-inch strips
1 pound (or less) Cheddar cheese, shredded

Rinse the chicken and pat dry. Arrange the chicken in a single layer in a large baking pan. Add the celery and chopped onion.

Bake, covered, at 375 degrees for 45 minutes.

Let cool. Debone the chicken and cut into bite-size pieces. Discard the celery and onion. Combine the chicken soup, mushroom soup, milk, grated onion, salsa and broth in a bowl and mix well.

Layer the chicken, tortilla strips and soup mixture $1/3$ at a time in a deep casserole or 9x13-inch baking dish. Top with the cheese. Chill, covered, for 24 hours.

Bake at 300 degrees for $1^{1}/_{2}$ to 2 hours or until cooked through.

If 2 cans of salsa are too hot, try 1 can salsa with 1 salsa can of milk.

Yield: 8 to 12 servings

Drunken Gamecock (Beer-Baked Chicken)

3 whole chicken breasts
4 to 5 tablespoons flour
Salt and pepper to taste
Vegetable oil
3 (10-ounce) cans cream of mushroom soup
2 tablespoons soy sauce
3/4 cup beer
2 (3-ounce) cans sliced mushrooms

Rinse the chicken and pat dry. Mix the flour, salt and pepper in a shallow dish. Dredge the chicken in the mixture. Heat the oil in a large skillet. Add the chicken. Cook until brown. Arrange the chicken in a shallow 9x13-inch baking pan. Mix the soup, soy sauce, beer and mushrooms in a bowl. Pour over the chicken.

Bake at 350 degrees for 1 hour, basting occasionally with the pan drippings.

Serve over pasta or rice.

Yield: 6 servings

Gator Gumbolaya

1 pound bacon
5 pounds boneless skinless chicken fillets
1 cup flour
1¼ cups vegetable oil
4 green bell peppers, chopped
5 pounds onions, chopped
2 bunches shallots, chopped
1 stalk celery, chopped
3 cans Dawn's mushroom steak sauce
2 cans tomatoes with green chiles
1 bottle Worcestershire sauce
1 (3-ounce) jar garlic powder, or to taste
1 (3-ounce) jar Italian seasoning, or to taste
6 cans chicken broth
4 cans beef broth
Salt and pepper to taste
MSG to taste
6 pounds lean pork cubes or chopped ham
6 pounds smoked sausage, cut into halves lengthwise, sliced

Gators love to travel to away games, and one of their favorite places is Baton Rouge for a Florida-LSU match-up. Tiger fans are great cooks and love to share their Cajun food with everyone (including us Gators). While tailgating before the game, this recipe was shared by Danny, Byron (Buz), and Kerry—three great Cajun chefs!

Fry the bacon in a large skillet until crisp. Crumble the bacon and set aside. Brown the chicken in the bacon drippings in the skillet. Add enough water to cover the chicken. Simmer until cooked through. Let cool. Cut the chicken into bite-size pieces and set aside.

Cook a mixture of the flour and oil in a large heavy skillet over medium heat until rich brown, stirring constantly; watch carefully to avoid burning. Add the green peppers, onions, shallots and celery. Cook until the vegetables are tender.

Pour the vegetable mixture into a large stockpot. Add the mushroom steak sauce, tomatoes, Worcestershire sauce, garlic powder, Italian seasoning, chicken broth, beef broth, salt, pepper and MSG and mix well. Simmer for 10 minutes. Add the chicken, pork cubes, bacon and sausage. Simmer for 2 hours.

Serve over rice. Recipe may be cut in half. May be prepared ahead and frozen.

Yield: 6 gallons

Honey Mustard Chicken Breasts à l'Orange

4 boneless skinless chicken breasts
1 teaspoon sage
Salt and pepper to taste
2 tablespoons honey
2 teaspoons vinegar
2 teaspoons Dijon mustard
1/3 cup orange juice
2 teaspoons chopped fresh parsley, or 1 teaspoon parsley flakes

Rinse the chicken and pat dry. Sprinkle with the sage, salt and pepper. Arrange in a single layer in a baking dish. Combine the honey, vinegar, Dijon mustard and orange juice in a bowl and mix well. Pour over the chicken. Sprinkle with the parsley.

Bake at 375 degrees for 35 to 45 minutes or until the chicken is cooked through.

To serve, spoon the sauce over the chicken.

Yield: **4 servings**

Oven-Baked Chicken with Honey Butter Sauce

$3/4$ cup flour
$3/4$ cup fine dry bread crumbs
$1^1/2$ teaspoons paprika
1 teaspoon salt
$1/2$ teaspoon pepper
8 boneless skinless chicken breasts
$1/4$ to $1/2$ cup melted butter
$1^1/2$ tablespoons vegetable oil
Honey Butter Sauce

Combine the flour, bread crumbs, paprika, salt and pepper in a zip-top plastic bag. Shake well to mix. Rinse the chicken and pat dry. Add 2 pieces of the chicken to the plastic bag at a time. Shake well to coat. Pour the butter and oil into a 9x13-inch baking dish. Add the chicken. Bake at 400 degrees for 30 minutes. Reduce the oven temperature to 350 degrees. Turn the chicken over. Bake for 20 to 25 minutes or until the chicken is cooked through. Serve with Honey Butter Sauce.

Yield: 8 servings

Honey Butter Sauce

$1/4$ cup butter
$1/4$ cup honey
$1/4$ cup lemon juice

Combine the butter, honey and lemon juice in a bowl and mix well.

Rosemary Chicken

This recipe was contributed by men's head basketball coach Billy Donovan. He played collegiately at Providence and was MVP in 1986 and 1987. He played professionally for the New York Knicks in 1987 and 1988.

 2 tablespoons chopped fresh rosemary, or 1 teaspoon dried
 Minced fresh garlic to taste
 1 tablespoon Dijon mustard
 1 tablespoon lemon juice
 Salt and pepper to taste
 2 tablespoons olive oil
 6 boneless chicken breasts

Combine the rosemary, garlic, Dijon mustard, lemon juice, salt, pepper and oil in a large bowl and mix well. Rinse the chicken and pat dry. Add to the rosemary mixture.

Marinate in the refrigerator for 30 minutes. Remove the chicken from the marinade, discarding the remaining marinade. Grill until the chicken is cooked through.

Yield: 4 servings

Craig Brown, Florida basketball

Smothered Italian Chicken

4 skinless chicken breasts
Salt and pepper to taste
Garlic salt to taste
Paprika to taste
Vegetable oil
1 medium onion, chopped
1 green bell pepper, chopped
1 small can mushrooms, drained
1 can stewed tomatoes
2 tablespoons cornstarch
Oregano to taste
4 slices provolone cheese

Rinse the chicken and pat dry. Sprinkle with salt, pepper, garlic salt and paprika. Pour a very small amount of vegetable oil into a large electric skillet or spray the skillet with nonstick cooking spray. Add the chicken. Cook until the chicken is brown. Remove to a plate.

Sauté the onion, green pepper and mushrooms in the skillet. Add the tomatoes. Thicken with a mixture of the cornstarch and a small amount of water. Pour into a bowl.

Return the chicken to the skillet. Sprinkle with oregano. Spoon the tomato mixture over the chicken.

Simmer, covered, for 45 to 60 minutes or until the chicken is cooked through. Place 1 slice of cheese over each chicken piece. Heat until the cheese melts.

Serve with yellow rice.

Yield: 4 servings

Storm Roberts' Tasty Tail-Gator Marinated Chicken

    10 to 15 large cloves of garlic
    1½ cups tarragon vinegar
    ¼ cup honey
    2 tablespoons vegetable oil
    2 tablespoons What's-this-here sauce (Worcestershire)
    4 teaspoons Grey Poupon mustard (any fancy French mustard will do;
        stay away from that Southern "yaller" stuff)
    3 to 4 pounds chicken breasts

Open a cold beer. Take a starter sip.

Place the garlic in a large zip-top plastic bag. Crush with a garlic press or the old-fashioned smash 'em way. Add the vinegar, honey, oil, Worcestershire sauce and mustard.

Take a sip of your beer.

Rinse the chicken and pat dry. Place in the plastic bag. Rub the marinade into the chicken and coat well. Let the chicken marinate in the refrigerator for at least 24 hours.

Finish your beer. You're done until time to grill.

Remove the chicken from the marinade. Grill until the chicken is cooked through, basting occasionally with the remaining marinade.

The garlic, vinegar and honey give this chicken a sweet glaze and unforgettable taste. It goes best with a Gator football victory.

Yield: 4 to 6 servings

Curry in a Hurry

2 onions, chopped
6 ribs celery, chopped
4½ tablespoons margarine
3 to 6 tablespoons curry powder
⅛ teaspoon powdered ginger
¼ cup flour
2 cups milk, or mixed milk and chicken broth
6 (10-ounce) cans cream of celery soup
12 chicken breasts, cooked, cut into bite-size pieces

Sauté the onions and celery in the margarine in a large skillet. Add the curry powder, ginger and flour and stir until smooth. Add the milk. Cook until thickened, stirring constantly. Add the soup.

Combine the cooked mixture with the chicken in a large bowl and mix well. Pour into a large lasagna pan or ovenproof bowl.

Bake at 350 degrees for 30 minutes or until heated through.

May be prepared ahead and frozen. Thaw before baking or heat, covered, at 350 degrees for 1 hour. Uncover and heat for 30 minutes longer or until hot.

Serve over rice with your choice of condiments, such as chopped egg whites, egg yolks, relish, chopped bacon, coconut, chopped black olives, chopped green olives, canned French-fried onion rings, raisins, chopped nuts and/or Major Grey's chutney.

Yield: 10 to 12 servings

River Chicken

This recipe was contributed by Neal Anderson.

6 to 8 skinless chicken pieces
1 (10- to 12-ounce jar) apricot preserves or light apricot preserves
1 (8-ounce) bottle Russian or Catalina salad dressing or light
  salad dressing
1 envelope onion soup mix

Rinse the chicken and pat dry. Place in an 8x12-inch baking dish. Mix the preserves, salad dressing and soup mix in a bowl. Pour over the chicken.

Bake, covered, at 325 to 350 degrees for 1 to 1¹/₂ hours or until the chicken is cooked through.

Serve over rice.

Yield: 4 to 6 servings

Neal Anderson scores again!

Herbed Chicken Casserole

3 pounds chicken breasts or other pieces
Flour
Salt and pepper to taste
3 tablespoons olive oil or vegetable oil
1 to 2 cloves of garlic, minced
6 to 8 small white onions, finely chopped
2 to 4 carrots, cut into thin shavings with a vegetable peeler
8 ounces mushrooms, sliced
2 cups dry red wine
2 tablespoons chopped parsley
1 to 2 bay leaves
$\frac{1}{4}$ teaspoon thyme

Rinse the chicken and pat dry. Combine the flour, salt and pepper in a zip-top plastic bag. Add the chicken and toss to coat. Brown the chicken in the oil in a skillet. Remove to a 2- to 3-quart casserole. Add the garlic to the skillet. Sauté for several minutes. Add the onions, carrots, mushrooms, wine, parsley and bay leaves, stirring to scrape up any brown bits. Pour over the chicken.

Bake at 350 degrees for 1 hour. Discard bay leaves before serving.

May add additional wine during baking for a thinner sauce. The sauce may be used over rice or thickened and served over mashed potatoes.

Yield: 6 to 8 servings

*Jill Craybas,
women's tennis*

Arroz con Pollo (Chicken and Rice)

This recipe was contributed by Andy Brandi, head coach of the women's tennis team.

  1 chicken, cut up
  Olive oil
  1 large clove of garlic, minced
  1 medium onion, chopped
  1/2 green bell pepper, chopped
  1 small can tomato sauce
  2 cans chicken broth
  Basil and oregano to taste
  Salt and pepper to taste
  Tabasco sauce to taste
  Saffron to taste
  2 cups cooked rice
  1 small can baby peas
  1 small jar chopped pimentos, drained

Rinse the chicken and pat dry. Brown the chicken in olive oil in a medium skillet. Remove and set aside.

Sauté the garlic lightly in olive oil in a large skillet. Add the onion and green pepper. Sauté until the vegetables are tender.

Add the tomato sauce, chicken broth, basil, oregano, salt, pepper, Tabasco sauce and saffron and mix well. Cook until heated through. Add the chicken. Cook for 30 minutes or until the chicken is cooked through. Stir in the rice, peas and pimentos.

May substitute pink beans for the peas and a small onion for the medium onion and omit the Tabasco sauce; cook over low heat for 15 minutes before adding the chicken.

Yield: 6 servings

Coach Holland's Chicken Tetrazzini

This recipe was contributed by Cathy Holland, wife of Lawson Holland and mother of Jake and Katie.

1 fryer, cut up, or 4 chicken breasts
2 tablespoons margarine
1 medium onion, chopped
2 tablespoons flour
½ cup milk
2 (10-ounce) cans cream of mushroom soup
1 small can mushrooms
1 tablespoon Worcestershire sauce
2½ to 3½ cups cooked spaghetti
1 cup shredded Cheddar cheese

Rinse the chicken. Combine with water to cover in a large saucepan. Boil until the chicken is cooked through; drain, reserving 1 cup stock. Allow the chicken to cool. Chop the chicken, discarding skin and bones; set aside.

Melt the margarine in a small skillet. Add the onion. Sauté until tender. Add the flour and milk and mix well.

Combine the onion mixture, chicken, soup, reserved stock, mushrooms, Worcestershire sauce and spaghetti in a bowl and mix well. Spoon into a 9x13-inch baking pan. Top with the cheese.

Bake at 350 degrees for 30 minutes.

Yield: 8 servings

Country-Style Chicken and Dumplings

3 cups flour
1½ teaspoons baking powder
1 tablespoon salt
1 stewing hen
1 tablespoon salt
½ teaspoon pepper
2 quarts water
1 egg, beaten

Mix the flour, baking powder and 1 tablespoon salt together and set aside. Rinse the chicken. Combine with 1 tablespoon salt, pepper and 1 quart of the water in a large saucepan. Cook until the chicken is tender and cooked through.

Remove the chicken from the saucepan and reserve the stock. Allow the chicken to cool. Cut into bite-size pieces, discarding skin and bones; set aside. Remove 1 cup reserved stock and set aside. Add the remaining 1 quart water to the reserved stock in the saucepan. Bring to a boil.

Mix the egg with the 1 cup reserved stock in a bowl. Add the flour mixture and mix well. Knead on a floured board until firm. Roll very thin and cut into the desired size.

Drop the dumplings into the boiling stock. Cook, covered, for 20 minutes. Add the chicken. Simmer until heated through.

Yield: 4 to 6 servings

Great Chicken Casserole

1 chicken, or 4 large chicken breasts
Salt to taste
1 package frozen broccoli or green peas
1 (10-ounce) can cream of mushroom soup
1/2 soup can milk
12 ounces Velveeta cheese, cubed
1 package vermicelli

Rinse the chicken. Combine with salt and water to cover in a saucepan. Boil until the chicken is tender; remove the chicken and reserve the broth. Cut the chicken into small pieces, discarding skin and bones. Cook the broccoli using the package directions, omitting the salt; drain.

Combine the soup, milk, 1 cup of the reserved broth and cheese in a saucepan. Cook over low heat until the cheese melts, stirring occasionally. Cook the vermicelli in the reserved broth in the saucepan until al dente. Combine the chicken, vermicelli, broccoli and cheese mixture in a bowl and mix well. Spoon into a large casserole.

Bake at 350 degrees for 30 minutes or until the chicken is cooked through.

Yield: 10 servings

Imperial Chicken

1 loaf bread, crusts trimmed
3/4 cup grated Parmesan or Romano cheese
1/2 teaspoon garlic powder
2 teaspoons salt
1/8 teaspoon pepper
1 chicken, cut into serving pieces
1/2 cup melted butter or margarine

Grate the bread into fine crumbs. Spread on a flat pan or tray. Let dry overnight. Combine the cheese, garlic powder, salt and pepper in a bowl and mix well. Add the bread crumbs.

Rinse the chicken and pat dry. Dip each piece into the butter, then into the crumb mixture. Arrange the chicken in a single layer in a roasting pan; do not overlap pieces. Drizzle with the remaining butter.

Bake at 350 degrees for 1 hour or until the chicken is cooked through. Do not turn the chicken during baking.

Yield: 5 servings

UF Degrees

*More than 100 majors in
94 undergraduate degrees
125 Master's programs
76 Doctoral programs
Professional post-baccalaureate
degrees in law, dentistry,
pharmacy, medicine, and
veterinary medicine*

Cabbage Chicken One-Dish Meal

1 large onion, chopped
2 to 3 tablespoons butter or margarine
1 small head cabbage, shredded
2 tablespoons garlic powder
2 packages ramen noodles soup mix
1 to 2 (5-ounce) cans chicken
Shredded cheese (optional)

Sauté the onion in the butter in a skillet. Stir in the cabbage and garlic powder. Cook until heated through.

Add the ramen noodles and seasoning packet. Add just enough water to moisten the noodles. Simmer, covered, for 10 to 15 minutes or until the cabbage is tender and the noodles are tender. Stir in the chicken. Add the cheese. Cook until the cheese melts.

Yield: 3 to 4 servings

Florida football is more than a sport. For hundreds of thousands of fans in the Sunshine State, it is an obsession. Their enthusiasm and loyalty, which they demonstrate time and time again, has elevated Florida football to a level where it unquestionably ranks as the most supported team in the state—indeed, among the most supported in all of college football. That support and interest still continues to grow and led to a 10,000-seat expansion of Ben Hill Griffin Stadium in 1991, which raised capacity to over 84,000 and elevated the Gator program to the highest echelon of support in the nation.

Chicken Casserole

$2^1/_2$ cups chopped cooked chicken
$^1/_4$ cup chopped celery
1 small onion, chopped
1 cup cooked rice
1 can chopped water chestnuts, drained
1 (10-ounce) can cream of chicken soup
$^3/_4$ cup mayonnaise
1 tablespoon lemon juice
1 teaspoon salt
Crushed butter crackers, crushed saltines or bread crumbs
$^1/_2$ cup melted butter

Combine the chicken, celery, onion, rice, water chestnuts, soup, mayonnaise, lemon juice and salt in a bowl and mix well. Spoon into a buttered 1-quart casserole. Top with the cracker crumbs. Drizzle the butter over the top.

Bake at 350 degrees for 30 minutes.

Yield: 6 servings

Honey-Gingered Pork Tenderloin

2 (12-ounce) pork tenderloins
1/4 cup honey
1/4 cup soy sauce
1/4 cup oyster sauce
2 tablespoons brown sugar
4 teaspoons minced fresh gingerroot
1 tablespoon minced garlic
1 tablespoon catsup
1/4 teaspoon onion powder
1/4 teaspoon ground red pepper
1/4 teaspoon ground cinnamon

Place the tenderloins in a 7x11-inch dish. Combine the honey, soy sauce, oyster sauce, brown sugar, gingerroot, garlic, catsup, onion powder, red pepper and cinnamon in a bowl and mix well. Pour over the tenderloins.

Marinate, covered, in the refrigerator for 8 hours, turning occasionally. Remove the tenderloins from the marinade, reserving the remaining marinade.

Grill the tenderloins over hot coals for 25 to 30 minutes or until a meat thermometer inserted in the thickest part of the tenderloins registers 160 degrees, turning frequently and basting with the marinade.

Slice thinly and arrange on a serving platter. Garnish with fresh parsley.

Yield: 4 to 6 servings

Amish Pork Chops

1 (10-ounce) can cream of mushroom soup
1 cup catsup
1 tablespoon Worcestershire sauce
1/2 cup chopped onion
6 pork loin chops

Mix the soup, catsup, Worcestershire sauce and onion in a bowl. Pour over the pork chops in an 11x14-inch baking dish. Bake at 350 degrees for 2 hours or until the pork chops are cooked through.

Yield: 4 servings

Pork Casserole

1 large can chicken-corn soup
1 1/2 cups prepared corn bread stuffing
1/4 cup chopped celery
1/4 cup chopped onion
1/2 teaspoon paprika
4 (3/4-inch-thick) boneless pork chops
1 tablespoon brown sugar
1 teaspoon spicy brown mustard

Mix the soup, stuffing, celery, onion and paprika in a bowl. Spoon into a greased 9-inch pie plate. Arrange the pork chops over the stuffing mixture. Sprinkle with a mixture of the brown sugar and mustard. Bake at 400 degrees for 30 minutes or until the pork chops are cooked through.

Yield: 4 servings

Gator Dogs

2 pounds lean ground beef or ground turkey
2 cups chili sauce
3 tablespoons chili powder
1 cup water
1 large potato, grated
24 hot dogs, boiled, grilled or fried
24 submarine sandwich buns
1 large onion, chopped
2 cups shredded Cheddar cheese

Brown the ground beef in a saucepan, stirring until crumbly; drain. Add the chili sauce, chili powder, water and potato. Simmer until thick.

Place the hog dogs in the buns. Spoon the ground beef mixture over the hot dogs. Top with the onion and cheese.

Yield: 24 servings

Champp Chow

This recipe was contributed by Chris Weaver, who was "Albert" from 1985 through 1987. He was featured as Albert in the 1986 Gator Bowl with Billy Crystal and in the book Glory Yards.

Creamed Seminole (1 cup white rice)
1 Tiger tail (1 kielbasa sausage, cut into halves)
Eyes of 100 Bulldogs (2 cans red kidney beans)
1/2 bean can water
Butter
Chopped Volun-"tears" (1 onion, chopped)

Cook the rice using the package directions. Pour just enough water into a large skillet to cover the bottom of the skillet. Add the sausage. Cook over medium heat for 15 minutes, turning occasionally; drain. Cook for 5 minutes longer or until brown on both sides.

Combine the beans and 1/2 bean can water in a saucepan. Cook over medium heat for 15 minutes. Cut the sausage into 2-inch pieces. Stir butter into the rice. Spoon the rice onto serving plates. Top each serving with sausage, beans and onion.

Serve with corn muffins or blueberry muffins.

Yield: 3 to 4 servings

Chris says, "I guess it was appropriate that I ate this New Orleans delicacy before the 1996 Championship Game in the Sugar Bowl. It's this Albert's favorite dinner."

Seafood Casserole

This recipe was contributed by Mary McCloskey, the mother of former "Albert" Chris Weaver.

4 ounces noodles, cooked
1 cup mayonnaise
1 cup sour cream
1 (10-ounce) can cream of mushroom soup
8 ounces cooked shrimp
8 ounces crab meat
1 (8-ounce) can mushrooms, drained (optional)
Shredded Cheddar cheese

Combine the noodles, mayonnaise, sour cream, soup, shrimp, crab meat and mushrooms in a bowl and mix well. Spoon into a 2-quart casserole. Top with cheese.

Bake at 350 degrees for 30 minutes.

Yield: 6 to 8 servings

Seafood and Pasta

6 tablespoons olive oil
36 large shrimp, peeled, deveined
$1/2$ cup butter
4 small cloves of garlic, minced
$1/2$ teaspoon seasoned salt
$1/2$ teaspoon freshly ground pepper
$1/8$ teaspoon cayenne
$1/2$ cup dry vermouth
6 tablespoons lemon juice
Cooked linguini or angel hair pasta
Creole seasoning (optional)

Heat the oil in a large skillet over medium heat. Add the shrimp. Cook until golden brown. Turn the shrimp and reduce the heat. Add the butter, garlic, seasoned salt, pepper and cayenne and mix well. Increase the heat to high.

Add the vermouth and lemon juice. Cook for 1 minute, stirring or shaking the skillet constantly. Spoon over linguini. Sprinkle with Creole seasoning.

May substitute scallops for the shrimp or use a mixture of shrimp and scallops.

Yield: 6 servings

Stuffed Grouper

This recipe was contributed by Bobby Raymond, former Gator placekicker.

Bobby Raymond not only ranks as UF's most accurate field goal kicker but also among the most accurate in collegiate history. His 97% conversion rate (32-33) for field goals under 40 yards was the best in NCAA history for a minimum of 30 career attempts.

> 2 pounds fresh skinless grouper fillets
> Sage Stuffing
> Melted butter or margarine
> 1 envelope Knorr's Swiss Hollandaise sauce mix
> 3 tablespoons lemon juice
> 3 drops of Tabasco sauce
> 4 teaspoons parsley flakes

Cut the fillets into 4 approximately 3-ounce pieces and 4 approximately 4-ounce pieces. Cut a 2-inch slit completely through the center of the larger pieces, creating a hole in the center. Place 3 ounces of the Sage Stuffing on each of the smaller pieces. Shape the stuffing into a ball. Top each with 1 of the larger pieces, pressing down so that the stuffing bulges through the slit. Place the fish in a glass baking dish. Add enough water to come 1/4 inch up the sides of the baking dish. Spoon butter over the fish. Bake at 350 degrees for 30 to 40 minutes or until the fish flakes easily. Prepare the sauce mix using the package directions and adding the lemon juice and Tabasco sauce. Remove the fish to serving plates. Spoon the Hollandaise sauce over each serving. Sprinkle with the parsley flakes.

Yield: 4 (10-ounce) servings

Sage Stuffing

> 1/2 loaf white bread
> 1 cup chopped celery
> 1 cup chopped onion
> 6 tablespoons butter or margarine
> 1/2 cup chopped walnuts
> 2 tablespoons crushed sage
> 4 teaspoons each poultry seasoning, salt and pepper
> 1 (10-ounce) can chicken stock

Tear the bread into small pieces and roll into coarse crumbs. Combine the celery, onion and butter in a sauté pan. Cook, covered, until the onion is tender and translucent. Add the bread crumbs, walnuts, sage, poultry seasoning, salt and pepper and mix well. Add enough of the chicken stock gradually to make the stuffing moist enough to shape into a ball. Season with additional sage, salt and pepper.

Black Bean and Cheese Tortilla Pie

1 (15-ounce) package all ready refrigerated pie pastry
3 tablespoons vegetable oil
1 cup chopped onion
$\frac{1}{2}$ cup chopped green or red bell peppers
1 (15-ounce) can black beans, drained
$\frac{1}{2}$ cup salsa
2 tablespoons minced fresh jalapeños (optional)
$\frac{1}{2}$ teaspoon chili powder (optional)
$\frac{1}{2}$ teaspoon cayenne (optional)
2 cups shredded Cheddar cheese
3 (8-inch) flour tortillas

Prepare the pie pastries using the package directions. Fit I pastry into a 9-inch pie plate or a 10-inch deep-dish pie plate.

Heat the oil in a large skillet over medium-high heat. Add the onion and green pepper. Cook for 5 minutes or until tender, stirring constantly. Add the beans, salsa, jalapeños, chili powder and cayenne. Simmer for 7 to 10 minutes or until heated through, stirring occasionally.

Spoon $\frac{1}{2}$ cup of the bean mixture into the pastry-lined pie plate. Sprinkle with $\frac{1}{2}$ cup of the cheese. Top with a tortilla. Repeat the layers twice. Sprinkle with the remaining $\frac{1}{2}$ cup cheese. Top with the remaining pie pastry, sealing and fluting the edge and cutting vents.

Bake at 350 degrees for 40 to 50 minutes or until brown.

Let stand for 10 minutes before slicing. May serve with sour cream.

Yield: 6 to 8 servings

Fresh Basil and Pepper Pasta

This recipe was contributed by John James, executive director of Gator Boosters.

1 (16-ounce) package corkscrew vegetable pasta
1 bunch green onions, chopped
1/3 cup water
1 (15-ounce) can garbanzo beans, drained, rinsed
1 (10-ounce) jar roasted red peppers, chopped
1/3 cup chopped fresh basil leaves
1 tablespoon drained capers
Freshly ground pepper to taste

Drop the pasta into a large pan of boiling water. Cook using the package directions.

Combine the green onions and 1/3 cup water in a saucepan. Cook for 2 minutes. Add the beans, roasted peppers, basil, capers and pepper and mix well. Cook for 5 minutes, stirring frequently.

Drain the pasta and place in a bowl. Pour the sauce over the pasta and mix well. Serve immediately.

Yield: 4 servings

Green Pizza

1 envelope pesto sauce mix
2 tablespoons olive oil
1/2 cup water
1 (10-ounce) package frozen spinach, thawed, drained
1 prepared pizza crust
8 ounces feta cheese, crumbled
4 cups shredded mozzarella cheese

Prepare the pesto sauce using the package directions, reducing the olive oil to 2 tablespoons and using 1/2 cup water. Mix the pesto sauce and spinach in a bowl. Spread over the pizza crust. Sprinkle the feta cheese over the spinach mixture. Top with the mozzarella cheese.

Bake at 425 degrees for 10 to 15 minutes or until the cheeses melt and are light brown. Cut into slices to serve.

Yield: 4 servings

Barbecue Sauce

2 tablespoons dark brown sugar
1 tablespoon white vinegar
1 tablespoon prepared mustard
1 cup catsup
1/2 cup water
1/4 teaspoon ground cinnamon, or to taste
1/8 teaspoon ground cloves, or to taste

Combine the brown sugar, vinegar, mustard, catsup, water, cinnamon and cloves in a saucepan. Bring to a boil over medium heat; reduce the heat. Simmer for 3 minutes. Serve warm or cold with pork or chicken.

Yield: 8 servings

Jezebel Sauce

1 (12-ounce) jar pineapple preserves
1 (10- to 12-ounce) jar apple jelly
1/4 teaspoon dry mustard
3 tablespoons horseradish
Coarsely ground pepper to taste

Mix the preserves, jelly, mustard, horseradish and pepper in a bowl. Adjust the seasonings. Store in the refrigerator until needed. Serve warm over ham.

Yield: 12 to 16 servings

Joe and Anita Tenuta's Secret Spaghetti Sauce

1 pound sausage, beef or pork cubes
Vegetable oil
5 cloves of garlic, pressed
2 small cans tomato paste, or 1 large can
4 (20-ounce) cans peeled tomatoes, crushed
Salt and pepper to taste
3 bay leaves
1 teaspoon fresh or dried basil
1 teaspoon sugar

Brown the sausage in oil in a skillet, stirring frequently; drain. Add the garlic. Cook until the garlic is light brown. Add the tomato paste. Cook for several minutes, stirring frequently. Add the tomatoes, salt, pepper, bay leaves, basil and sugar and mix well. Simmer for 2^1/$_2$ to 3 hours. Remove and discard the bay leaves. Serve the sauce over hot cooked spaghetti.

Yield: 16 to 24 servings

Vegetables & Side Dishes

Sidelines

Green Bean Casserole

1/2 cup chopped onion
1/2 cup chopped celery
1/4 cup margarine
1 (11-ounce) can Shoe Peg corn
1 (14-ounce) can green beans
1 (10-ounce) can cream of celery soup
1 cup sour cream
1/4 cup shredded Cheddar cheese
1 cup (about) crushed butter crackers

Sauté the onion and celery in the margarine in a skillet. Combine the celery mixture, corn, beans, soup, sour cream and cheese in a bowl and mix well. Pour into a 2^{1}/2-quart casserole. Top with the cracker crumbs.

Bake at 350 degrees for 30 minutes.

Yield: 8 servings

Pictured on page 119, Albert and Alberta.

Tex-Mex Beans

    3 (15-ounce) cans kidney beans, drained, rinsed
    1 cup chopped celery
    1/2 cup chopped green bell pepper
    1/2 cup chopped onion
    1 cup chopped tomato
    1 (4-ounce) can green chiles, chopped
    2 cups shredded Cheddar cheese
    2 teaspoons chili powder
    1 teaspoon salt
    1 cup mayonnaise
    1 cup crushed tostada chips

Combine the beans, celery, green pepper, onion, tomato, green chiles, cheese, chili powder, salt and mayonnaise in a bowl and mix well. Pour into an 8x12-inch baking dish. Top with the crushed chips.

Bake at 350 degrees for 40 minutes.

May be prepared 1 day ahead and stored in the refrigerator; baking time may need to be lengthened.

Yield: 6 to 8 servings

Broccoli Casserole

1 bunch fresh broccoli, chopped
1 (10-ounce) can light cream of mushroom soup
1 (10-ounce) can light cream of chicken soup
2 tablespoons flour
1 cup sour cream
$1/2$ cup grated carrot
2 tablespoons grated onion
$1/2$ teaspoon salt
$1/4$ teaspoon pepper
$1^1/2$ cups herb-seasoned stuffing mix
$1/4$ cup melted margarine

Cook the broccoli in water to cover in a saucepan until tender; drain. Combine the soups, flour, sour cream, carrot, onion, salt and pepper in a bowl and mix well. Stir in the broccoli.

Mix the stuffing mix with the margarine in a medium bowl. Stir $1/2$ cup of the stuffing into the broccoli mixture. Spoon into a 4-quart casserole. Top with the remaining stuffing.

Bake, covered, at 350 degrees for 30 minutes or until heated through.

Yield: 6 to 8 servings

Woodport Broccoli Casserole

This recipe was contributed by Ward Pell, wife of former head football coach Charley Pell.

    6 packages frozen broccoli
    2 large onions, chopped
    1/2 cup butter
    4 (10-ounce) cans cream of mushroom soup
    3 packages garlic cheese
    1 large can sliced mushrooms
    1 cup blanched almonds
    1 cup toasted bread crumbs

Cook the broccoli using the package directions; do not overcook. Sauté the onions in the butter in a skillet. Add the soup, cheese, mushrooms and 3/4 cup of the almonds.

Drain the broccoli and add to the onion mixture. Pour into a 9x13-inch casserole. Top with the bread crumbs.

Bake at 300 degrees for 15 minutes or until bubbly and heated through.

Yield: 15 servings

Ward Pell recalls, "This recipe was 'borrowed' from Woodport, a lovely old plantation in Hartfield, Virginia, when we were coaching at Virginia Tech. Fitzhugh and Elsie Moore had a dinner party to introduce us to other Golden Hokies and served us this wonderful casserole. Not being a fan of broccoli (like former President Bush), I learned to love it after tasting this version."

Broccoli with Cheese Casserole

2 (10-ounce) packages frozen chopped broccoli
Salt to taste
1 (10-ounce) can cream of mushroom soup
1 cup mayonnaise
2 eggs, beaten
1 cup shredded sharp Cheddar cheese
1/4 cup chopped sweet onion
1/2 cup crushed butter crackers
1/4 cup butter

Cook the broccoli in boiling salted water to cover in a saucepan for 5 minutes; drain. Combine the soup, mayonnaise, eggs, cheese and onion in a bowl. Add the broccoli and mix well. Pour into a 9x13-inch baking dish or a shallow 3-quart baking dish. Top with the crushed crackers. Dot with the butter.

Bake at 350 degrees for 30 minutes or until the top is light brown.

Yield: 8 to 12 servings

Cheesy Baked Broccoli

2 (10-ounce) packages frozen broccoli or asparagus
2 tablespoons flour
$1/2$ teaspoon salt
2 tablespoons melted butter
$3/4$ cup milk
1 cup shredded Cheddar cheese
Crushed cheese crackers or bread crumbs

Cook the broccoli using the package directions. Mix the flour and salt in a saucepan. Stir in the butter. Add the milk and cheese. Cook over low heat until the cheese melts. Drain the broccoli. Combine with the cheese mixture in a bowl. Pour the broccoli mixture into a baking dish. Sprinkle with the crushed crackers.

Bake at 350 degrees for 15 to 20 minutes or until heated through.

Yield: 8 servings

Ruth's Confetti Corn Casserole

1 (15-ounce) can whole kernel corn or Mexicorn, drained
1 (15-ounce) can cream-style corn
1 small package corn bread mix
1 cup sour cream
1 (2-ounce) jar chopped pimentos
3 to 4 slices bacon, crisp-fried, crumbled (optional)
Pepper to taste

Combine the whole kernel corn, cream-style corn, corn bread mix, sour cream, pimentos, bacon and pepper in a bowl and mix well. Pour into an 8x8-inch baking pan sprayed with nonstick cooking spray.

Bake at 350 degrees for 1 hour.

Yield: 6 to 8 servings

Carlton Bruner, U.S. Senior National Champion 1500 m freestyle, 1992, 1993

Gator Taters Twenty-Seven Ways

4 baking potatoes or sweet potatoes
2 tablespoons vegetable oil
1/4 teaspoon salt

Cut the potatoes into 3-inch-long shoestring strips, thin steak fry wedges or extra-thin chip slices. Season with your choice of the following: 1 tablespoon chili powder, 1 tablespoon ground cinnamon and 1 tablespoon cumin; 2 tablespoons prepared horseradish and 1/4 cup Dijon mustard; or 2 tablespoons chopped parsley, 2 tablespoons sage and 2 minced cloves of garlic.

Toss shoestring or steak-cut potatoes with the oil; coat chips with nonstick cooking spray instead. Place in a baking pan.

Bake at 350 degrees for 10 minutes or until golden brown, turning occasionally. Sprinkle with the salt.

Serve with your choice of the following sauces: 1 cup salsa and 1/4 cup plain yogurt; 1 cup plain yogurt and 2 tablespoons chopped dill; or 1 cup mixed mustard and mayonnaise.

Yield: 8 servings

Parmesan Potatoes

$\frac{1}{2}$ cup butter or margarine
$\frac{1}{4}$ cup flour
$\frac{1}{2}$ cup grated Parmesan cheese
1 teaspoon salt
$\frac{1}{8}$ teaspoon pepper, or to taste
4 or 5 large potatoes, peeled, cut into 1-inch chunks

Melt the butter in a 9x11-inch glass baking dish. Mix the flour, cheese, salt and pepper in a zip-top plastic bag. Add the potatoes and shake to coat. Spread the potatoes in the prepared baking dish.

Bake at 375 degrees for 1 hour, turning once with a spatula.

Yield: 6 servings

Page Dunlap, Florida golf

Potatoes Romanoff

6 cups cubed potatoes
2 cups large curd cottage cheese
1 cup sour cream
1 clove of garlic, minced
1 teaspoon salt
2 tablespoons chopped chives
1 cup shredded Cheddar cheese
Paprika to taste

Boil the potatoes in water to cover in a saucepan until tender; drain. Combine the potatoes, cottage cheese, sour cream, garlic, salt and chives in a bowl and mix well. Pour into a buttered casserole. Top with the cheese and sprinkle with paprika.

Bake at 350 degrees for 25 to 30 minutes or until heated through.

May be prepared ahead and stored in the refrigerator for several days before baking.

Yield: 8 to 10 servings

Baked Potato Casserole

8 potatoes, cooked, peeled, cubed
1 pound American cheese, cut into strips
1 cup mayonnaise
1/2 cup chopped onion
Salt and pepper to taste
8 ounces bacon, crisp-fried, crumbled
1/2 cup sliced pimento-stuffed olives

Combine the potatoes, cheese, mayonnaise, onion, salt and pepper in a bowl and mix well. Pour into a 9x13-inch baking pan. Top with the bacon and olives.

Bake at 325 degrees for 1 hour.

Yield: 12 servings

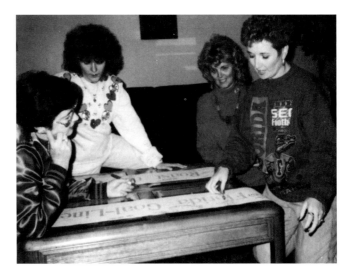

Goal-Liners sign Spirit Banner.

Scalloped Potatoes

2 teaspoons grated onion
3 tablespoons melted butter
3 tablespoons flour
1½ cups milk
1½ teaspoons salt
⅛ teaspoon cayenne, or to taste
1 cup (or more) shredded Cheddar cheese
¾ cup shredded green bell pepper
¾ cup chopped pimentos
4 cups thinly sliced potatoes

Sauté the onion in the butter in a skillet. Stir in the flour. Cook until heated through. Add the milk gradually, stirring constantly. Season with salt and cayenne. Bring to a boil, stirring until smooth; reduce the heat. Add the cheese, green pepper and pimentos.

Alternate layers of the potatoes and cheese sauce in a greased 1½-quart baking dish until all the ingredients are used.

Bake, covered, at 350 degrees for 30 minutes. Bake, uncovered, for 1½ hours longer.

Yield: 6 servings

Mom's Casserole

1 package frozen spinach or broccoli
1 (10-ounce) can cream of celery soup
1/4 cup mayonnaise
1 egg, beaten
3/4 cup Italian bread crumbs
1/4 cup chopped onion
3/4 cup shredded Cheddar cheese
1 teaspoon salt
1 1/2 teaspoons pepper

Cook the spinach using the package directions; drain. Mix the soup, mayonnaise, egg and bread crumbs in a bowl. Add the spinach, onion, half the cheese, salt and pepper and mix well. Pour into a 7x7-inch glass baking dish.

Bake at 350 degrees for 30 minutes. Remove from the oven and stir. Bake for 40 minutes. Sprinkle with the remaining cheese. Bake for 5 minutes longer.

May be microwaved at 80 percent power for 14 minutes, stirring after 8 minutes; sprinkle with the remaining cheese during the last 2 minutes cooking time. Let stand for 3 to 5 minutes. Serve hot.

Yield: 8 servings

Squash and Water Chestnut Casserole

    6 tablespoons butter
    15 to 20 saltines, crushed
    2 tablespoons vegetable oil
    2 medium onions, finely chopped
    2 to 3 cups drained cooked yellow squash
    1 (10-ounce) can cream of chicken soup
    1 cup sour cream
    1 (8-ounce) can thinly sliced or chopped water chestnuts, drained

Melt the butter in a large skillet. Add the cracker crumbs and mix well. Pour into a small bowl.

Heat the oil in the skillet. Add the onions. Sauté until tender. Add the squash, soup, sour cream, water chestnuts and $3/4$ of the crumbs and mix well. Pour into a 2-quart casserole. Sprinkle with the remaining crumbs.

Bake at 350 degrees for 25 to 30 minutes or until the top is golden brown.

Yield: 8 servings

Yellow Squash Casserole

12 ounces Colby cheese
2 pounds yellow squash, sliced
2 medium or large onions, sliced
$\frac{1}{4}$ cup melted butter or margarine
3 or 4 eggs, beaten
1 small can evaporated milk
1 sleeve butter crackers, crushed
Salt and pepper to taste

Shred a small amount of the cheese; cut the remaining cheese into cubes. Boil the squash and onions in water to cover in a saucepan until tender; drain. Combine the squash mixture and butter in a large bowl and mix well.

Beat the eggs and evaporated milk in a medium bowl. Add to the squash mixture. Add the cubed cheese, most of the cracker crumbs, salt and pepper. Pour into a 9x13-inch casserole. Top with the shredded cheese and remaining cracker crumbs.

Bake at 350 degrees for 40 minutes.

Yield: 8 to 10 servings

Charley's Sweet Potato Casserole

This recipe was contributed by Ward Pell, wife of former head football coach Charley Pell. The first time Charley prepared this, he used recipes from two cookbooks and combined the ingredients he thought sounded good!

3 cups cooked sweet potatoes
3/4 cup sugar
1/2 cup butter
2 eggs
1 teaspoon vanilla extract
1/3 cup evaporated milk
1 (1-pound) package light brown sugar
1/2 cup self-rising flour
1 cup chopped pecans
1/2 cup melted butter

Mix the sweet potatoes, sugar, 1/2 cup butter, eggs, vanilla and evaporated milk in a bowl. Pour into a 9x13-inch casserole. Mix the brown sugar, flour, pecans and 1/2 cup butter in a bowl until crumbly. Sprinkle over the sweet potato mixture. Bake at 325 degrees for 25 to 30 minutes or until heated through. Any excess topping mixture can be stored, covered, in the refrigerator; heat and use as ice cream topping.

Yield: 10 servings

Charley Pell became UF head coach in 1979, and his last four teams went to bowls, averaging eight wins a season against one of the nation's most demanding schedules. Pell's 1983 team secured the school's then highest final ranking ever with a number 6 finish. Wilber Marshall, a linebacker, was named National Defensive Player of the Year. Other top players of the Pell era (1979-84) were WR Cris Collinsworth, LB David Little, DT David Galloway, and OT Lomas Brown. All were first-team All-America selections.

Ward and Charley Pell with gift of appreciation from Florida Goal-Liners

Candied Sweet Potatoes

This recipe was contributed by Jane Edmondson, wife of George Edmondson ("Mr. Two Bits," a Florida cheerleading fixture for 49 years).

6 to 8 medium sweet potatoes
1½ cups sugar
¾ cup butter
¾ cup water
½ teaspoon salt
¼ cup corn syrup
Juice of 1 lemon

Boil the sweet potatoes in water to cover in a saucepan just until tender. Peel and cut into slices. Place in a casserole.

Bring the sugar, butter, water and salt to a boil in a saucepan. Add the corn syrup. Cook for 5 minutes; remove from the heat. Add the lemon juice and mix well. Pour over the sweet potatoes.

Bake at 350 degrees for 1 hour.

May cook and peel the sweet potatoes 1 day ahead; store in the refrigerator.

Yield: 6 to 8 servings

Sweet Potato Casserole

2 eggs
$\frac{1}{2}$ cup butter, softened
$\frac{1}{4}$ cup milk
1 large can sweet potatoes, drained, mashed
1 cup sugar
1 teaspoon vanilla extract
$\frac{1}{2}$ cup butter, softened
1 cup shredded coconut
1 cup sugar
$\frac{1}{2}$ cup self-rising flour

Combine the eggs, $\frac{1}{2}$ cup butter, milk, sweet potatoes, I cup sugar and vanilla in a mixer bowl and beat well. Pour into a buttered 2-quart baking dish.

Mix $\frac{1}{2}$ cup butter, coconut, I cup sugar and flour in a bowl until crumbly. Sprinkle over the sweet potato mixture.

Bake at 350 degrees for I hour or until bubbly and heated through.

Yield: 6 to 8 servings

Absolutely Scrumptious Sweet Potato Casserole

3 cups mashed cooked sweet potatoes
1 cup sugar
2 eggs
1 teaspoon vanilla extract
$1/2$ cup skim milk
$1/4$ cup butter
1 cup packed brown sugar
$1/2$ cup flour
$1/3$ cup butter
1 cup chopped pecans

Combine the sweet potatoes, sugar, eggs, vanilla, skim milk and $1/4$ cup butter in a large bowl and mix well. Spoon into a greased 8x8-inch square baking dish or 2-quart casserole.

Combine the brown sugar, flour, $1/3$ cup butter and pecans in a bowl and mix until crumbly. Sprinkle over the sweet potato mixture.

Bake at 350 degrees for 30 minutes.

Yield: 6 to 8 servings

Brandy Sweet Potatoes

3 pounds sweet potatoes, cooked, peeled
1/2 cup butter
1 cup packed light brown sugar
1/2 cup brandy
1/2 teaspoon cinnamon
1/4 teaspoon nutmeg
1/4 teaspoon salt
1 (20-ounce) can pineapple chunks in syrup, drained
3/4 cup chopped walnuts

Cut the sweet potatoes into chunks and set aside. Melt the butter in a large saucepan. Add the brown sugar, brandy, cinnamon, nutmeg and salt. Cook over high heat for 4 minutes or until the liquid is reduced to a syrup. Add the sweet potatoes. Cook until the sweet potatoes are glazed.

Pour into a 3-quart casserole, reserving 1/4 cup of the syrup. Arrange the pineapple over the top. Sprinkle with the walnuts. Pour the reserved syrup over the top.

Bake at 375 degrees for 15 minutes or until heated through.

Yield: 8 to 12 servings

Italian Zucchini

1$\frac{1}{2}$ pounds zucchini
1 onion, chopped
Salt to taste
1 egg
1$\frac{1}{2}$ tablespoons butter
$\frac{1}{2}$ teaspoon poppy seeds
$\frac{1}{2}$ teaspoon garlic salt
$\frac{1}{2}$ teaspoon pepper
Grated Parmesan cheese to taste

Scrub and slice the zucchini. Combine the zucchini, onion and salted water to cover in a saucepan. Boil gently until tender. Drain in a colander.

Combine the zucchini mixture, egg, butter, poppy seeds, garlic salt and pepper in a bowl and mix well. Pour into a baking dish. Sprinkle with cheese.

Bake at 375 degrees for 30 minutes.

Yield: 6 servings

Peg's Zucchini Casserole with Sausage

This recipe was contributed by Ann Marie Rogers, associate athletic director of women's sports.

2 pounds zucchini
1 pound bulk sausage
1/4 cup chopped onion, or to taste
1 clove of garlic, minced
2 eggs, lightly beaten
1 cup soft bread crumbs
1/4 cup grated Parmesan cheese
1 teaspoon thyme, or to taste
1/2 teaspoon salt, or to taste
1/4 teaspoon oregano, or to taste
1/4 cup grated Parmesan cheese

Cook the zucchini in boiling salted water to cover in a saucepan for 10 to 15 minutes or until tender. Drain by squeezing the moisture from the zucchini. Chop coarsely and set aside.

Combine the sausage, onion and garlic in a skillet. Cook over medium heat until brown, stirring until the sausage is crumbly; drain.

Combine the zucchini, sausage mixture, eggs, bread crumbs, 1/4 cup cheese, thyme, salt and oregano in a bowl and mix well. Pour into a shallow baking dish. Sprinkle with 1/4 cup cheese.

Bake at 325 to 350 degrees for 45 minutes.

Yield: 6 servings

Under Ann Marie Rogers' guidance, the UF program has finished among the ten most successful women's programs in the nation in each of the last 11 years. Seven out of nine years, the women's program has won the All-SEC Women's All Sports Trophy. This year marks the celebration of the twenty-fifth anniversary of women's athletics at UF.

Dirty Rice

1 pound ground beef
1 pound bulk sausage
1 onion, chopped
2 to 3 ribs celery, chopped
Salt and pepper to taste
1/2 teaspoon red pepper flakes
3 cups rice, cooked

Combine the ground beef, sausage, onion, celery, salt and pepper in a large skillet. Cook until the ground beef and sausage are brown and crumbly, stirring frequently; drain.

Add the red pepper and enough water to make of a soupy consistency. Add the rice. Simmer for 15 to 20 minutes or until heated through. Adjust the seasonings.

Yield: 8 to 10 servings

Broccoli Rice

1 large onion, chopped
3 tablespoons butter or margarine
1 (10-ounce) can cream of chicken soup
1/2 cup milk
8 ounces Velveeta cheese, chopped
1/2 cup long grain rice, cooked
1 (10-ounce) package frozen chopped broccoli
1/4 teaspoon garlic seasoning (optional)
Pepper to taste

Sauté the onion in the butter in a large skillet. Add the soup, milk and cheese. Cook until the cheese melts.

Combine the cheese mixture, rice, broccoli, garlic seasoning and pepper in a bowl and mix well. Pour into a 2-quart baking dish.

Bake at 350 degrees for 25 minutes or until heated through.

Yield: 8 servings

Gator Beans and Rice

4 (15-ounce) cans black beans
1 small onion, chopped
1 tablespoon butter or margarine
¼ teaspoon garlic powder
1 large package Success rice

Drain 2 cans of the beans, reserving the liquid. Purée the drained beans and reserved liquid with a hand blender. Sauté the onion in the butter in a skillet.

Combine the puréed beans, onion, garlic powder and 2 cans undrained beans in a saucepan. Cook until heated through. Cook the rice using the package directions.

Serve the beans over the rice.

Yield: 4 to 6 servings

Red Rice

1 large can tomatoes
6 slices bacon
1 green bell pepper, chopped
1 medium onion, chopped
1 cup rice
1 teaspoon sugar
Salt and pepper to taste

Drain the tomatoes, reserving the liquid. Combine the reserved liquid with enough water to measure 2 cups. Purée the tomatoes and set aside.

Cook the bacon in a medium saucepan until crisp. Crumble the bacon and set aside.

Sauté the green pepper and onion in the bacon drippings. Add the rice, stirring until coated. Add the water mixture, puréed tomatoes, sugar, salt and pepper and mix well.

Bring to a boil. Simmer, covered, for 20 to 30 minutes or until the liquid is absorbed.

Let stand, covered, for 15 minutes or until the rice is fluffy. Stir in the bacon.

Yield: 6 to 8 servings

Scalloped Pineapple

This recipe belonged to Vida Alexander, a Goal-Liner from 1979 until her death in 1995.

1 cup sugar
1 can crushed pineapple, drained
¼ cup milk
½ cup melted butter
3 eggs, lightly beaten
6 slices bread, cubed

Combine the sugar, pineapple, milk, butter, eggs and bread cubes in a bowl and mix well. Pour into a greased baking dish.

Bake at 350 degrees for 40 minutes.

May be served as a dessert.

Yield: 6 servings

Cece's Cream of Chicken Gravy

2 (10-ounce) cans cream of chicken soup
3/4 soup can water
1 small can mushroom halves, drained
Chopped cooked chicken or turkey giblets (optional)
2 hard-cooked eggs, sliced (optional)

Combine the soup and water in a saucepan. Add the mushrooms and chicken giblets. Bring to a simmer. Add the eggs.

Serve over corn bread dressing.

Yield: 6 to 8 servings

Mark Marklein, 1993 NCAA doubles champion, men's tennis

Breads

Gators on the Rise

Banana Nut Bread

2 cups flour
1 teaspoon baking soda
$^1/_2$ teaspoon salt
$^1/_2$ cup vegetable oil
1 cup sugar
2 eggs
3 bananas, mashed
1 teaspoon vanilla extract
3 tablespoons milk
1 cup chopped pecans or walnuts

Mix the flour, baking soda and salt together. Combine the oil, sugar, eggs and bananas in a large bowl. Add the flour mixture and mix well. Add the vanilla, milk and pecans and mix well. Pour into a greased loaf pan.

Bake at 350 degrees for 1 hour.

Yield: 12 servings

Pumpkin Bread

3½ cups self-rising flour
1 teaspoon baking powder
½ teaspoon ground cloves
1 teaspoon cinnamon
1 teaspoon nutmeg
1 teaspoon allspice
3 cups sugar
4 eggs, beaten
1 cup vegetable oil
1 can pumpkin
⅔ cup water

Mix the flour, baking powder, cloves, cinnamon, nutmeg and allspice together. Combine the sugar, eggs and oil in a large bowl. Add the pumpkin and mix well. Add the flour mixture and mix well. Stir in the water. Pour into 3 greased and waxed paper-lined loaf pans.

Bake at 350 degrees for 45 to 50 minutes or until the loaves test done.

Yield: 36 servings

Corn Bread

1¼ cups flour
¾ cup cornmeal
¼ cup sugar
2 teaspoons baking powder
½ teaspoon salt
1 cup skim milk
¼ cup vegetable oil
2 eggs

Combine the flour, cornmeal, sugar, baking powder and salt in a bowl. Stir in the milk, oil and eggs and mix just until moist. Pour into a greased 8x9-inch baking pan, muffin cups or ovenproof skillet.

Bake at 400 degrees for 20 to 25 minutes or until brown.

Yield: 9 servings

Gator helmet

Mexican Corn Bread

2 eggs
1 tablespoon baking powder
1/3 cup vegetable oil
1 1/2 teaspoons salt
1 cup cream-style corn
1 cup sour cream
1 cup yellow cornmeal
1 can small jalapeños or green chiles, seeded, chopped
1 cup shredded Cheddar cheese

Mix the eggs, baking powder, oil, salt, corn, sour cream and cornmeal in a bowl. Pour half the batter into a greased large cast-iron skillet. Place the jalapeños over the batter. Sprinkle with half the cheese. Pour the remaining batter over the cheese. Top with the remaining cheese.

Bake at 350 degrees for 1 hour.

Yield: 6 to 8 servings

Broccoli Corn Bread

1 package frozen chopped broccoli, thawed, drained
1 large onion, chopped
6 ounces cottage cheese
$\frac{1}{2}$ cup melted margarine
4 eggs, beaten
1 teaspoon salt
2 small packages corn bread mix

Mix the broccoli, onion, cottage cheese, margarine, eggs and salt in a bowl. Add the corn bread mix and mix well. Pour into a greased 9x13-inch baking pan.

Bake at 400 degrees for 30 minutes.

Yield: 6 to 8 servings

Herbert Perry, Florida baseball

Best Corn Bread

    1 small package corn bread mix
    1 package white corn bread mix
    1 (16-ounce) can cream-style corn
    1 cup sour cream
    2 eggs, lightly beaten
    1/2 cup milk
    1/2 cup vegetable oil

Combine the corn bread mixes, corn, sour cream, eggs, milk and oil in a large bowl and mix well. Pour into a greased 2-quart casserole.

Bake at 350 degrees for 30 to 35 minutes or until the center is set.

Yield: 8 servings

Cinnamon Buns

1 envelope dry yeast
3/4 cup warm (110 to 115 degrees) water
1/4 cup shortening
1/4 cup sugar
1 egg
2 1/4 cups sifted self-rising flour
Softened butter
Cinnamon to taste
Sugar to taste

Dissolve the yeast in the warm water in a mixer bowl. Add the shortening, 1/4 cup sugar, egg and 1 cup of the flour. Beat at medium speed for 2 minutes, scraping the bowl frequently. Stir in the remaining flour and mix well, scraping side of bowl frequently.

Cover with a cloth and let rise in a warm place for 1 hour or until doubled in bulk. Stir down by beating for 25 strokes.

Turn the dough onto a floured cloth-covered board. Roll into a 9x12-inch rectangle. Spread with butter. Sprinkle with cinnamon and additional sugar.

Roll up from the wide side, pinching the edges to seal. Cut into 12 slices. Place in a greased 9x9-inch baking pan. Let rise in a warm place until doubled in bulk.

Bake at 375 degrees for 40 minutes or until brown.

Yield: 12 servings

Mother's Yeast Rolls

1/2 cup sugar
2 teaspoons salt
6 tablespoons vegetable oil
1 1/2 cups scalded milk
1 package yeast
1/2 cup lukewarm water
2 eggs, lightly beaten
6 1/2 cups flour
Melted butter

Mix the sugar, salt and oil in a large bowl. Add the milk. Set aside to cool to lukewarm. Dissolve the yeast in the lukewarm water. Add to the eggs in a bowl and mix well. Add the egg mixture to the milk mixture. Add half the flour and beat until smooth. Work in the remaining flour.

Place the dough in a greased bowl. Chill, covered, overnight. Roll out on a floured surface. Cut with a biscuit cutter. Spread with butter. Fold the rolls in half. Place in nonstick baking pans. Let rise for 3 hours.

Bake at 425 degrees for 8 to 10 minutes or until brown.

Yield: **36 servings**

Bojangle's Biscuits

3 cups self-rising flour
1 tablespoon confectioners' sugar
1 tablespoon baking powder
$1/2$ cup shortening
$1^1/2$ cups buttermilk
Melted butter

Mix the flour, confectioners' sugar and baking powder in a bowl. Stir in the shortening until crumbly. Add the buttermilk, stirring quickly until the dough pulls away from the side of the bowl.

Turn onto a floured board. Knead for 5 minutes. Roll $1/2$ inch thick. Cut with a $3^1/2$-inch biscuit cutter. Dip each biscuit into butter. Place on a greased baking sheet.

Bake at 400 degrees for 10 to 15 minutes or until brown.

Yield: **12 servings**

Sweet Potato Biscuits

2 cups self-rising flour
1/4 cup sugar
3 tablespoons shortening
2 tablespoons butter, softened
1 cup mashed cooked sweet potatoes
1/3 cup milk

Combine the flour and sugar in a bowl. Cut in the shortening and butter until crumbly. Add the sweet potatoes and milk and mix just until moist.

Turn the dough onto a lightly floured surface. Knead 4 to 5 times. Roll 1/2 inch thick. Cut with a 2-inch biscuit cutter. Place on lightly greased baking sheets.

Bake at 400 degrees for 15 minutes or until golden brown.

Yield: 18 servings

Florida's overall men's sports program has captured 74 Southeastern Conference championships.

Angel Biscuits

1 package dry yeast
5 tablespoons warm water
5 cups flour
5 teaspoons baking powder
$\frac{1}{2}$ teaspoon baking soda
$\frac{1}{2}$ teaspoon salt
1 cup shortening
2 cups buttermilk

Dissolve the yeast in the water and set aside. Sift the flour, baking powder, baking soda and salt into a bowl. Cut in the shortening. Add the yeast and buttermilk and mix by hand.

Turn onto a floured board. Roll with a floured rolling pin. Cut with a biscuit cutter. Place on nonstick baking sheets.

Bake at 400 degrees for 10 to 12 minutes or until golden brown.

Yield: 25 servings

Cheese Garlic Biscuits

2 cups buttermilk baking mix
2/3 cup milk
1 cup shredded Cheddar cheese
1/4 cup melted butter
1/2 teaspoon garlic powder
1 tablespoon parsley flakes

Combine the baking mix, milk and cheese in a bowl. Mix until a soft dough forms. Drop by spoonfuls onto a nonstick baking sheet.

Bake at 450 degrees for 10 minutes or until light brown.

Mix the butter, garlic powder and parsley flakes in a bowl. Brush over the warm biscuits on the baking sheet. Serve warm.

Yield: 12 servings

Cookies & Candy

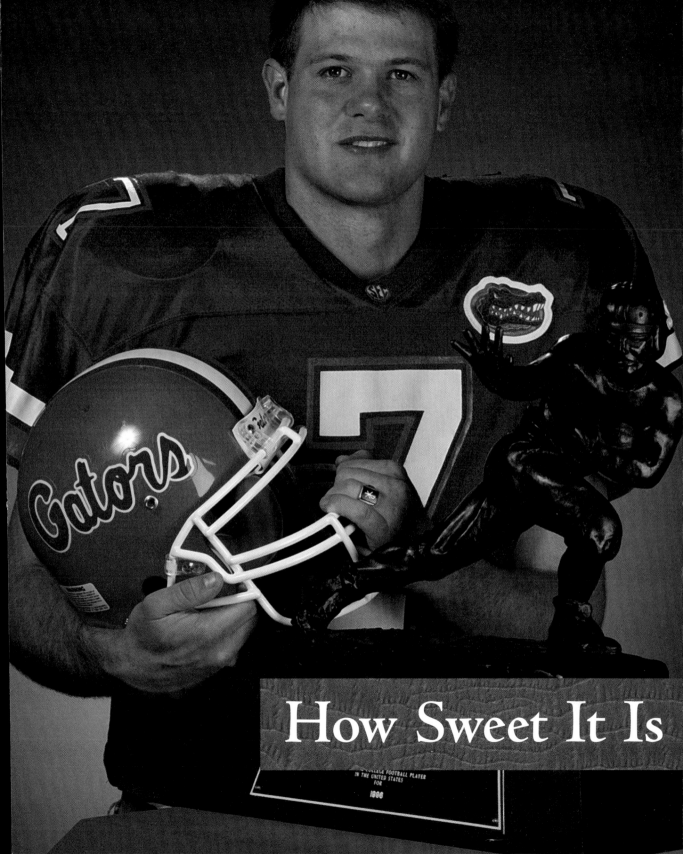

How Sweet It Is

Cashew Cheese Wafers

1 pound sharp Cheddar cheese, shredded
1 cup butter, softened
Salt to taste
1/4 teaspoon cayenne
2 cups flour
2 cups finely chopped cashews
Paprika, onion powder or cayenne to taste

Beat the cheese in a mixer bowl until creamy. Add the butter, beating constantly. Add the salt and cayenne. Add the flour 3 tablespoons at a time, beating constantly until a soft dough forms. Add the cashews and mix well. Shape into small balls. Place on a cookie sheet and flatten with a floured fork.

Bake at 325 degrees for 20 to 25 minutes or until brown.

Sprinkle paprika over the warm cookies. Store in an airtight container.

Yield: 2 dozen

Pictured on page 163,
Danny Wuerffel and his
1996 Heisman Trophy.

Chocolate Mint Cookies

16 ounces dark chocolate in microwave-safe container
¼ to ½ teaspoon peppermint extract
45 to 50 butter crackers

Melt the chocolate using the package directions. Stir until smooth. Add the flavoring and mix well. Coat each cracker with the chocolate mixture. Place on waxed paper to dry.

Yield: 45 to 50 servings

Some faithful Goal-Liners gather at the goal line before the 1997 Orange & Blue game.

Chocolate Tempters

3 cups quick-cooking oats
1/4 cup coconut
2 cups sugar
1/2 cup baking cocoa
1/2 cup milk
1/2 cup butter
1/2 cup peanut butter
1 teaspoon vanilla extract

Combine the oats and coconut in a large bowl. Combine the sugar, baking cocoa, milk and butter in a medium saucepan. Bring to a boil, stirring constantly. Boil for 1 minute.

Add the peanut butter and vanilla, stirring until smooth. Pour over the oat mixture and mix well. Drop by spoonfuls onto waxed paper. Let stand until firm. Store in an airtight container.

Yield: 2 to 3 dozen

Date Balls

1 pound chopped dates
1 cup margarine
1 cup sugar
4½ cups crisp rice cereal
1 cup chopped pecans or walnuts
1 (1-pound) package confectioners' sugar

Combine the dates, margarine and sugar in a large heavy saucepan or skillet. Cook for 2 to 5 minutes or until the mixture is bubbly and the margarine melts. Remove from the heat. Add the cereal and pecans. Shape into small balls. Sprinkle with confectioners' sugar while warm.

Yield: 6 dozen

Gator Chomps

3½ cups flour
1 teaspoon baking soda
½ teaspoon salt
1 cup butter or margarine, softened
1 cup sugar
1 cup packed brown sugar
1 egg
1 cup vegetable oil
1 teaspoon vanilla extract
1 cup rolled oats
1 cup crushed cornflakes
½ cup flaked coconut
1 cup chopped pecans

Mix the flour, baking soda and salt together. Cream the butter in a mixer bowl until light and fluffy. Add the sugar and brown sugar, beating well at medium speed.

Add the egg and beat well. Add the oil and vanilla and beat well. Add the flour mixture gradually, beating well after each addition. Stir in the oats, cornflakes, coconut and pecans. Shape into 1-inch balls. Place on nonstick cookie sheets. Flatten with a fork.

Bake at 325 degrees for 15 minutes.

Cool slightly. Remove to wire racks to cool completely.

Yield: 10 to 12 dozen

Suzy's Meringue Cookies

2 egg whites
$\frac{1}{8}$ teaspoon cream of tartar
$\frac{1}{8}$ teaspoon salt
$\frac{1}{4}$ teaspoon vanilla or almond extract
$\frac{1}{2}$ cup sugar
12 ounces miniature chocolate chips, or 1 cup chopped pecans

Beat the egg whites, cream of tartar, salt and vanilla in a mixer bowl until soft peaks form. Add the sugar gradually, beating constantly until stiff peaks form. Fold in the chocolate chips. Drop by teaspoonfuls onto parchment-lined cookie sheets.

Bake at 250 degrees for 20 to 25 minutes or until dry.

Cool until slightly warm. Remove to a wire rack.

Yield: 2$\frac{1}{2}$ dozen

John J. Tigert, University of Florida President from 1928-1947, co-founder of the Southeastern Conference and creator of the athletic grant-in-aid program used in the NCAA today, once said, "I believe that athletics are a part of the true college education program. They teach what cannot be learned in the classroom."

Oatmeal Raisin Cookies

1½ cups flour
1 teaspoon baking soda
1 teaspoon salt (optional)
1½ teaspoons cinnamon
½ teaspoon nutmeg
1¼ cups butter, softened
¾ cup packed brown sugar
½ cup sugar
1 egg
1½ teaspoons vanilla extract
3 cups rolled oats
½ cup flaked coconut
1 cup raisins

Mix the flour, baking soda, salt, cinnamon and nutmeg together. Cream the butter, brown sugar and sugar in a mixer bowl until light and fluffy. Beat in the egg and vanilla.

Add the flour mixture and mix well. Stir in the oats, coconut and raisins. Drop onto a nonstick cookie sheet.

Bake at 350 degrees for 10 to 12 minutes or until brown.

Yield: 4 dozen

Grandma's Persimmon Cookies

This recipe was contributed by Cathryn Lombardi, First Lady of the University of Florida. Cathryn holds a botany degree and at one point was a cartographer. She has taught math and biology in Venezuela and is active in many community organizations.

    1 cup persimmon pulp
    1 cup packed brown sugar
    1 cup shortening
    2 cups flour
    1 teaspoon salt
    1 teaspoon cinnamon
    1 teaspoon baking soda
    1 egg
    1 teaspoon vanilla extract
    1 cup walnut pieces
    1 cup raisins

Combine the persimmon pulp, brown sugar, shortening, flour, salt, cinnamon, baking soda, egg, vanilla, walnuts and raisins in a large bowl and mix well. Drop by teaspoonfuls onto a lightly greased cookie sheet.

Bake at 350 degrees for 10 minutes.

Yield: 2 dozen

Toffee Crisps

This recipe was contributed by Becky Burleigh, the University of Florida's first women's soccer coach. She led the team to a perfect (8-0) league record in 1996 and was named SEC Coach of the Year. She was a four-year letter winner at Methodist College.

1 cup sugar
1/2 cup packed brown sugar
1/2 cup butter or margarine, softened
1 teaspoon vanilla extract
2 eggs
2 1/4 cups flour
1 teaspoon baking powder
1/2 teaspoon baking soda
1/2 teaspoon salt
1 cup almond brickle chips

Cream the sugar, brown sugar and butter in a mixer bowl until light and fluffy. Add the vanilla and eggs and beat well.

Add the flour, baking powder, baking soda and salt and beat well. Stir in the almond brickle chips. Drop by rounded teaspoonfuls 2 inches apart onto cookie sheets sprayed with nonstick cooking spray.

Bake at 375 degrees for 8 to 12 minutes or until light golden brown.

Remove from the cookie sheets immediately.

Yield: 6 dozen

Greek Wedding Cookies

    1 cup margarine, softened
    1 cup shortening
    1 cup sugar
    4 cups sifted flour
    4$\frac{1}{2}$ teaspoons vanilla extract
    1 cup chopped pecans
    2 cups confectioners' sugar

Whip the margarine, shortening and sugar in a large bowl. Add the flour gradually, mixing until the dough is very stiff. Add the vanilla and pecans. Shape into small balls. Place on lightly greased cookie sheets.

Bake at 350 degrees for 8 to 10 minutes or until the bottoms of the cookies are light brown. Overbaking will cause the cookies to become hard.

Drop the warm cookies into the confectioners' sugar in a paper bag. Shake until coated. Cool on wire racks.

Yield: 4 dozen

Whitney White, Gator women's soccer

White Chocolate Chip Cookies

2 cups flour
3/4 cup baking cocoa
1 teaspoon baking soda
1/2 teaspoon salt
1 cup butter, softened
2 cups sugar
2 eggs
2 teaspoons vanilla extract
1 2/3 cups white chocolate chips

Mix the flour, baking cocoa, baking soda and salt together. Beat the butter and sugar in a mixer bowl until creamy. Add the eggs and vanilla. Beat until light and fluffy.

Add the flour mixture gradually, beating well after each addition. Stir in the white chocolate chips. Drop by rounded teaspoonfuls onto a nonstick cookie sheet.

Bake at 350 degrees for 8 to 9 minutes.

Cool slightly. Remove to a wire rack to cool completely. These cookies will puff and be soft while baking; they will flatten upon cooling.

Yield: 4 1/2 dozen

Blonde Brownies

5 1/3 cups sifted flour
5 teaspoons baking powder
1 teaspoon salt
1 1/2 cups butter
2 (1-pound) packages light brown sugar
6 extra-large eggs
2 cups chopped pecans
2 cups semisweet chocolate chips

Sift the flour, baking powder and salt together. Melt the butter in a large saucepan. Stir in the brown sugar. Let cool for 10 minutes or longer. Beat in the eggs 1 at a time. Stir in the flour mixture, pecans and chocolate chips. Spread in a greased 12x17-inch baking pan.

Bake at 350 degrees for 30 to 35 minutes or until the center springs back when lightly touched.

Yield: 6 dozen

Dale's Favorite Butterscotch Brownie Bars

1/2 cup vegetable oil
2 tablespoons water
2 eggs
1 (2-layer) package yellow cake mix
2 cups miniature marshmallows
1 cup butterscotch, peanut butter or chocolate chips

Combine the oil, water and eggs in a small bowl and mix well. Add to the cake mix in a large bowl and mix well. Stir in the marshmallows. Add the butterscotch chips and mix well. Spread in a 9x13-inch baking pan sprayed with nonstick cooking spray.

Bake at 325 degrees for 40 to 45 minutes or until the brownies spring back when lightly touched.

Let cool. Cut into 2-inch bars.

Yield: 15 to 20 servings

Caramel Brownies

1 cup flour
2 teaspoons baking powder
1/2 teaspoon salt
2 cups packed light brown sugar
1/2 cup plus 2 tablespoons melted butter
2 eggs, beaten
2 teaspoons vanilla extract
1 cup chopped pecans or walnuts

Sift the flour, baking powder and salt together. Combine the brown sugar, butter, eggs, vanilla and pecans in a large bowl. Add the flour mixture and mix well. Spread in a nonstick 9x13-inch baking pan.

Bake at 325 degrees for 40 to 50 minutes or until a wooden pick inserted near the center comes out clean.

Let cool. Cut into squares.

Yield: 15 servings

Gator Stomp Brownies

1 (2-layer) package German chocolate cake mix
1 cup chopped pecans
$1/3$ cup evaporated milk
$3/4$ cup melted butter
1 (14-ounce) package vanilla caramels
$1/2$ cup evaporated milk
1 cup semisweet chocolate chips

Mix the cake mix, pecans, $1/3$ cup evaporated milk and butter in a bowl. Press half the mixture into a greased 9x13-inch baking dish.

Bake at 350 degrees for 8 minutes.

Heat the caramels and $1/2$ cup evaporated milk in a double boiler until the caramels melt, stirring occasionally. Pour over the baked layer. Cover with the chocolate chips. Top with the remaining pecan mixture.

Bake at 350 degrees for 18 minutes.

Let cool. Cut into squares.

Yield: 15 servings

Butter Pecan Turtle Cookies

2 cups flour
1 cup packed brown sugar
$\frac{1}{2}$ cup butter
1 cup pecan halves
$\frac{2}{3}$ cup butter
$\frac{1}{2}$ cup packed brown sugar
1 cup milk chocolate chips

Combine the flour, 1 cup brown sugar and $\frac{1}{2}$ cup butter in a 3-quart mixer bowl. Beat at medium speed for 2 to 3 minutes or until fine particles form, scraping bowl frequently. Pat into a nonstick 9x13-inch baking pan. Sprinkle with the pecans.

Combine $\frac{2}{3}$ cup butter and $\frac{1}{2}$ cup brown sugar in a heavy 1-quart saucepan. Bring to a boil over medium heat, stirring constantly. Boil for 1 minute, stirring constantly. Pour evenly over the pecans and flour mixture in the pan.

Bake at 350 degrees for 18 to 22 minutes or until set. Remove from the oven.

Sprinkle with the chocolate chips immediately. Swirl the chocolate chips slightly as they melt, leaving some whole for a marbled effect. Do not spread the chocolate.

Let cool. Cut into bars. May be frozen after baking.

Yield: 3 to 4 dozen

Lemon Squares

1 (2-layer) package lemon cake mix
½ cup melted butter or margarine
1 egg, beaten
1 (1-pound) package confectioners' sugar
8 ounces cream cheese, softened
2 eggs
1 teaspoon lemon juice
Confectioners' sugar

Mix the cake mix, butter and 1 egg in a bowl. Press into a greased 9x12-inch baking pan. Set aside a small amount of the confectioners' sugar. Combine the cream cheese, 2 eggs, remaining confectioners' sugar and lemon juice in a bowl and mix well. Pour over the cake mix mixture.

Bake at 350 degrees for 20 to 25 minutes or until golden brown.

Let cool. Chill for several hours. Sprinkle with the reserved confectioners' sugar. Cut into small squares.

Recipe may be doubled and baked in a larger pan.

Yield: 15 servings

Peanut Butter Cups

½ cup melted margarine
1 cup smooth or crunchy peanut butter
1½ cups graham cracker crumbs
1 cup chocolate chips

Combine the margarine, peanut butter and graham cracker crumbs in a bowl and mix well. Press into a 9x13-inch dish. Melt the chocolate chips in a microwave or double boiler. Spread over the peanut butter mixture. Chill for 30 minutes or longer. Cut into squares.

Yield: 15 servings

Seven-Layer Cookies

This recipe was contributed by Ward Pell, wife of former head football coach Charley Pell.

1/2 cup melted butter
1 cup graham cracker crumbs
1 cup grated coconut
1 cup butterscotch chips
1 cup chocolate chips
1 can sweetened condensed milk
1 cup chopped pecans

Pour the butter into a 9x13-inch baking pan. Layer the graham cracker crumbs, coconut, butterscotch chips, chocolate chips, condensed milk and pecans in the pan.

Bake at 350 degrees for 30 minutes.

Cool completely before cutting into squares.

Yield: 32 servings

Scotcheroos

  1 cup sugar
  1 cup light corn syrup
  1 cup peanut butter
  6 cups crisp rice cereal
  1 package chocolate chips
  1 package butterscotch chips

Bring the sugar and corn syrup to a boil in a saucepan. Stir in the peanut butter. Add the cereal and mix well. Press into a greased pan.

Melt the chocolate chips and butterscotch chips in a double boiler. Spread over the cereal mixture. Chill completely. Cut into bars.

Yield: 2 to 3 dozen

Propelled by its five SEC championships in 1995-96, Florida completed a sweep of all three SEC All-Sports titles— capturing the 1995-96 overall title, as well as finishing first in the men's and women's all-sports competition.

Swamp Bars

1/2 cup butter
1 1/2 cups graham cracker crumbs
1 cup chocolate chips
1 cup butterscotch chips
1 1/2 cups flaked coconut
1 cup chopped pecans
1 (14-ounce) can sweetened condensed milk

Melt the butter in a 9x13-inch baking pan. Sprinkle the graham cracker crumbs in the pan. Top with the chocolate chips, butterscotch chips, coconut and pecans. Press down gently. Pour the condensed milk over the top.

Bake at 350 degrees for 25 to 30 minutes or until set.

Let cool for 10 minutes. Cut into squares.

Yield: 15 servings

Tiny Toffee Squares

1 cup butter, softened
1 cup packed dark brown sugar
1 egg
1 teaspoon vanilla extract
2 cups flour, sifted
1/2 teaspoon salt
1/2 pound milk chocolate, melted
1/2 cup chopped pecans or walnuts

Cream the butter and brown sugar in a mixer bowl until light and fluffy. Beat in the egg. Add the vanilla, flour and salt and mix well. Spread evenly in a nonstick 10x15-inch baking pan.

Bake at 350 degrees for 25 minutes.

Top with the chocolate. Sprinkle with the pecans. Cut into small squares while warm. Cool in the pan.

Yield: 2 dozen

Pecan Kisses

1 egg white
1/8 teaspoon salt
3/4 cup packed light brown sugar
1/2 teaspoon vanilla extract
2 to 3 cups pecan halves

Beat the egg white and salt in a mixer bowl until stiff peaks form. Fold in the brown sugar and vanilla. Dip the pecan halves into the mixture. Place on a baking sheet sprayed with nonstick cooking spray.

Bake at 250 degrees for 30 minutes.

Turn off the oven. Let stand in the closed oven for 30 minutes.

Yield: 15 to 20 servings

Women's softball, inaugural season

Sugared Pecans

¹/₂ cup sugar
¹/₄ teaspoon salt
¹/₂ teaspoon cinnamon
¹/₄ teaspoon nutmeg
1 egg white
1 tablespoon water
2 cups pecans

Mix the sugar, salt, cinnamon and nutmeg in a bowl. Beat the egg white and water in a mixer bowl until frothy. Add the pecans, stirring until coated. Add the sugar mixture and mix well. Pour onto a buttered baking sheet.

Bake at 300 degrees for 30 minutes, stirring every 10 minutes.

Remove to a plate to cool. Break into pieces. Store in an airtight container.

Yield: 15 to 20 servings

Marshmallow Fudge

2 cups sugar
2 ounces chocolate
$^2/_3$ cup whipping cream
$^1/_2$ cup butter
18 marshmallows, or 6 tablespoons marshmallow creme
1 cup chopped pecans or walnuts
1 teaspoon vanilla extract

Combine the sugar, chocolate, whipping cream and butter in a saucepan. Add the marshmallows. Bring to a boil. Boil for 5 minutes. Add the pecans, stirring constantly.

Let stand to cool slightly for several minutes. Beat in the vanilla until the surface is no longer glossy. Spread in a buttered dish.

Yield: **36 servings**

Gator Delight Greased Lightning Fudge

1 teaspoon butter or margarine, softened
1 (16-ounce) package chocolate cream drops
1 cup smooth or crunchy peanut butter

Spread the butter in a 9x9-inch pan. Microwave the chocolate drops in a glass bowl on High for 2 minutes, stirring after 1 minute. Stir in the peanut butter. Spread in the prepared pan. Let stand until cool. Cut into squares.

Yield: 12 servings

Florida Goal-Liners sponsor senior homecoming float.

Desserts

End Zone

Apple Cake

2½ cups sifted flour
1 teaspoon baking soda
¾ teaspoon salt
¾ teaspoon cinnamon
1½ cups sugar
¾ cup margarine, softened
2 eggs
¾ cup warm coffee or water
3 cups chopped apples
Chopped walnuts (optional)
½ cup packed brown sugar
½ teaspoon cinnamon

Pictured on page 191, University of Florida Century Tower.

Sift the flour, baking soda, salt and ¾ teaspoon cinnamon together. Cream the sugar and margarine in a mixer bowl until light and fluffy. Beat in the eggs.

Add the flour mixture and coffee alternately to the creamed mixture, beating well after each addition. Stir in the apples and walnuts. Pour into a greased 8x12-inch cake pan. Sprinkle with a mixture of the brown sugar and ½ teaspoon cinnamon.

Bake at 350 degrees for 45 minutes.

Yield: 12 to 15 servings

Carrot Cake with Cream Cheese Frosting

2 cups flour
1 tablespoon baking soda
2 teaspoons cinnamon
1/2 teaspoon salt
2 cups sugar
1 1/2 cups vegetable oil
3 cups grated carrots
4 eggs
1 teaspoon vanilla extract
1 1/2 cups chopped walnuts or pecans
Cream Cheese Frosting

Mix the flour, baking soda, cinnamon and salt together. Cream the sugar and oil in a mixer bowl until light and fluffy. Add the carrots and beat well. Beat in the eggs 1 at a time. Add the flour mixture gradually, beating well after each addition. Stir in the vanilla and walnuts. Pour into a greased 9x13-inch cake pan. Bake at 300 degrees for 45 to 60 minutes or until a wooden pick comes out clean. Spread with Cream Cheese Frosting. May be baked in 2 round cake pans.

Yield: 20 servings

Cream Cheese Frosting

1/2 cup butter, softened
8 ounces cream cheese, softened
1 (1-pound) package confectioners' sugar
1 teaspoon vanilla extract (optional)

Cream the butter and cream cheese in a mixer bowl until light and fluffy. Add the confectioners' sugar gradually, beating constantly until of spreading consistency. Beat in the vanilla.

Chewy Cake

1/2 cup margarine, softened
1 (16-ounce) package light brown sugar
3 eggs
2 tablespoons vanilla extract
2 cups self-rising flour
2 cups chopped pecans
1/2 to 1 can flaked coconut

Combine the margarine, brown sugar, eggs and vanilla in a bowl and mix well. Add the flour, pecans and coconut and mix well. Pour into a greased and floured 9x13-inch cake pan.

Bake at 350 degrees for 30 to 35 minutes or until the edges pull away from the pan.

Yield: 15 servings

Dionne Rose, 1992 Lady Gators, track and field

Better-Than-Sex Cake

    1 cup semisweet chocolate chips
    3/4 cup chopped pecans
    1 (2-layer) package chocolate butter-recipe cake mix
    4 eggs
    1/2 cup vegetable oil
    1 teaspoon vanilla extract
    1 (4-ounce) package chocolate instant pudding mix
    1 cup sour cream

Toss the chocolate chips and pecans with 1 tablespoon of the cake mix.

Combine the remaining cake mix, eggs, oil, vanilla, pudding mix and sour cream in a mixer bowl. Beat for 3 minutes. Fold in the chocolate chip mixture. Pour into a greased and floured bundt pan or tube pan.

Bake at 350 degrees for 50 minutes or until a wooden pick inserted near the center comes out clean.

Yield: 12 servings

Easy Fudge Cherry Cake with Chocolate Frosting

1 (2-layer) package fudge cake mix
1 (21-ounce) can cherry pie filling
1 teaspoon almond extract
2 eggs, beaten, or equivalent amount of egg substitute
Chocolate Frosting

Grease and flour a 9x13-inch cake pan or spray with nonstick baking spray. Combine the cake mix, pie filling, flavoring and eggs in a bowl and mix well. Pour into the prepared pan. Bake at 350 degrees for 40 minutes. Spread with Chocolate Frosting.

Yield: 12 to 14 servings

Chocolate Frosting

5 tablespoons butter or margarine
1 cup sugar
1/3 cup milk
1 cup semisweet chocolate chips

Bring the butter, sugar and milk to a boil in a saucepan, stirring constantly. Remove from the heat. Stir in the chocolate chips. Beat until smooth.

Chocolate Cake with Creamy Chocolate Frosting

1 cup butter, softened
1/4 cup baking cocoa
1 cup water
2 cups sugar
2 cups flour
2 eggs
1 teaspoon baking soda
1/2 cup buttermilk
1 teaspoon vanilla extract
Creamy Chocolate Frosting

Combine the butter, baking cocoa and water in a saucepan. Cook until the butter melts, stirring occasionally. Combine the cocoa mixture, sugar and flour in a large bowl and mix well. Add the eggs, baking soda, buttermilk and vanilla and mix well. Pour into a greased and floured 9x13-inch cake pan. Bake at 350 degrees for 30 minutes. Cool on a wire rack. Spread with Creamy Chocolate Frosting.

Yield: 12 servings

Creamy Chocolate Frosting

1/2 cup butter
5 tablespoons milk
1/4 cup baking cocoa
1 (1-pound) package confectioners' sugar

Melt the butter in a saucepan. Add the milk and baking cocoa. Add the confectioners' sugar gradually, mixing until of spreading consistency. Let cool before using.

Chocolate Pound Cake

This recipe was contributed by Errophene Crozier, wife of Orville Crozier, a UF football player in 1928.

> 1¹/₂ cups butter, softened
> 3 cups sugar
> 5 eggs
> 3 cups flour, sifted
> 1 tablespoon vanilla extract
> 5 tablespoons baking cocoa, sifted
> 1 to 1¹/₄ cups milk

Cream the butter in a mixer bowl until light and fluffy. Add the sugar and mix well. Beat in the eggs 1 at a time. Add the flour and vanilla.

Add the baking cocoa and milk alternately to the creamed mixture, beating well after each addition. Pour into a tube pan sprayed with nonstick cooking spray.

Bake at 300 degrees for 1¹/₂ hours.

Cool in the pan for 15 minutes. Invert onto a serving plate.

Yield: 16 servings

Chocolate Kahlúa Pound Cake

1 (2-layer) package pudding-recipe devil's food cake mix
1/2 cup sugar
1/3 cup vegetable oil
3 eggs
3/4 cup water
1/4 cup bourbon
1/2 cup Kahlúa
3/4 cup strong black coffee
2 teaspoons baking cocoa
Chocolate Chip Icing

Combine the cake mix, sugar, oil, eggs, water, bourbon, Kahlúa, coffee
and baking cocoa in a mixer bowl. Beat for 4 minutes. Pour into a buttered
bundt pan. Bake at 350 degrees for 50 minutes. Cool in the pan for 10
minutes. Invert onto a serving plate. Pour Chocolate Chip Icing over
the cake.

Yield: 16 servings

Chocolate Chip Icing

1/4 cup butter
1 cup sugar
1/3 cup evaporated milk
1 cup chocolate chips

Combine the butter, sugar and evaporated milk in a saucepan. Boil for
2 minutes, stirring constantly. Remove from the heat. Add the chocolate
chips, stirring until smooth and adding additional evaporated milk
if needed.

German Chocolate Upside Down Cake

1 cup shredded coconut
1 cup chopped pecans
1 (2-layer) package German chocolate cake mix
1/2 cup margarine, softened
8 ounces cream cheese, softened
1 (1-pound) package confectioners' sugar

Place the coconut and pecans in a nonstick 9x13-inch cake pan. Prepare the cake mix using the package directions. Pour over the coconut and pecans. Mix the margarine, cream cheese and confectioners' sugar in a bowl. Pour over the batter or drop by dollops onto the batter.

Bake at 350 degrees for 35 minutes.

Cool completely. Serve upside down.

Yield: 15 servings

Charley's Favorite Coconut Cake

This recipe was contributed by Ward Pell, wife of former head football coach Charley Pell.

> 1 (2-layer) package yellow cake mix
> 1 (4-ounce) package vanilla instant pudding mix
> 1⅓ cups water
> 4 eggs
> ¼ cup vegetable oil
> 2 cups flaked coconut
> 1 cup chopped walnuts
> Coconut Cream Frosting
> 1 cup browned coconut (see Coconut Cream Frosting below)

Combine the cake mix, pudding mix, water, eggs and oil in a large mixer bowl. Beat at medium speed for 4 minutes. Stir in 2 cups coconut and walnuts. Pour into 3 greased and floured 9-inch round cake pans. Bake at 350 degrees for 35 minutes. Remove to a wire rack to cool. Spread Coconut Cream Frosting between the layers and over the top and side of the cake. Sprinkle with the browned coconut.

Yield: 12 servings

Coconut Cream Frosting

> ¼ cup butter
> 4 cups flaked coconut
> ¼ cup butter, softened
> 16 ounces cream cheese, softened
> 4 teaspoons milk
> 7 cups sifted confectioners' sugar
> 1 teaspoon vanilla extract

Melt ¼ cup butter in a skillet. Add 4 cups coconut. Cook over low heat until golden brown, stirring constantly. Spread on a paper towel to cool. Cream ¼ cup butter and cream cheese in a mixer bowl until light and fluffy. Add the milk and confectioners' sugar alternately, beating well after each addition. Add the vanilla. Stir in 3 cups browned coconut.

Cranberry Pecan Pound Cake

This recipe was contributed by Opal Graves, wife of Roy Graves, UF's head football coach from 1960-1969. He holds the record for most wins (70) by a head coach in school history.

1 cup chopped pecans
1¼ cups all-purpose flour
1 cup cake flour
½ teaspoon salt
2 cups sugar
1 cup unsalted butter, softened
5 large eggs
¼ cup sour cream
¼ cup Triple Sec, Grand Marnier or other orange-flavored liqueur
2 teaspoons vanilla extract
1 teaspoon grated orange peel
1½ cups coarsely chopped cranberries

Spread the pecans on a baking sheet. Bake at 350 degrees for 10 minutes or until lightly colored and fragrant. Sift the all-purpose flour, cake flour and salt together.

Cream the sugar and butter in a mixer bowl until light and fluffy, scraping the side of the bowl once. Beat in the eggs 1 at a time. Beat in the sour cream. Beat in the liqueur, vanilla and orange peel.

Add the flour mixture gradually, beating at low speed after each addition. Fold in the pecans and cranberries. Pour into a buttered and floured 2½-quart tube pan or bundt pan. Tap the pan on the counter to release any air bubbles.

Bake at 350 degrees for 1 hour or until a wooden pick inserted near the center comes out clean.

Cool in the pan for 10 minutes. Invert onto a wire rack to cool completely. Chill, wrapped in plastic, for 1 to 3 days before serving. May toast slices before serving.

Yield: 16 servings

Gator Bait Italian Cream Cake

2 cups sifted flour
1 teaspoon baking soda
2 cups sugar
1 cup shortening
1/2 cup margarine, softened
5 egg yolks
1 tablespoon vanilla extract
1 cup buttermilk
2 cups flaked coconut
1 cup chopped pecans
5 egg whites, stiffly beaten
1/2 cup margarine, softened
8 ounces cream cheese, softened
1 (1-pound) package confectioners' sugar
1 teaspoon vanilla extract
1/4 to 1/2 cup chopped pecans (optional)

Sift the flour and baking soda together. Cream the sugar and shortening in a mixer bowl. Add 1/2 cup margarine and beat until light and fluffy.

Beat in the egg yolks 1 at a time. Add 1 tablespoon vanilla, buttermilk and flour mixture alternately, beating well after each addition. Stir in the coconut and 1 cup pecans. Fold in the egg whites. Pour into 3 greased and floured cake pans.

Bake at 350 degrees for 30 minutes.

Combine 1/2 cup margarine and cream cheese in a mixer bowl. Beat until creamy. Add the confectioners' sugar gradually, beating until of spreading consistency. Add 1 teaspoon vanilla. Stir in 1/4 cup pecans. Spread between the layers and over the top and side of the cake.

Yield: 12 servings

Hummingbird Cake

3 cups flour
2 cups sugar
1 teaspoon salt
1 teaspoon baking soda
1 teaspoon cinnamon
3 eggs, beaten
1½ cups vegetable oil
1½ teaspoons vanilla extract
1 (8-ounce) can crushed pineapple
1 cup chopped pecans or walnuts
2 cups chopped bananas
1 cup butter or margarine, softened
16 ounces cream cheese, softened
2 cups confectioners' sugar
2 teaspoons vanilla extract
1 cup chopped pecans or walnuts

Combine the flour, sugar, salt, baking soda and cinnamon in a large bowl and mix well. Add the eggs and oil, mixing just until moist. Add 1½ teaspoons vanilla, undrained pineapple, 1 cup pecans and bananas. Spoon into a greased 9x13-inch cake pan.

Bake at 350 degrees for 25 to 30 minutes or until the cake tests done.

Cream the butter and cream cheese in a mixer bowl. Add the confectioners' sugar, beating until light and fluffy. Stir in 2 teaspoons vanilla and 1 cup pecans. Spread over the cooled cake.

Yield: 15 servings

Date Nut Cake

1 cup flour
1 tablespoon baking powder
1 teaspoon salt
1 quart pecans, finely to medium chopped
3 eggs
1 cup sugar
1/2 cup pineapple juice
1 teaspoon vanilla extract
1 teaspoon almond extract
16 ounces chopped pitted dates
1/2 to 1 cup Grand Marnier

Mix most of the flour, baking powder and salt together. Coat the pecans with the remaining flour. Beat the eggs and sugar in a mixer bowl. Add the flour mixture and pineapple juice alternately, beating well after each addition. Add the flavorings. Stir in the pecans and dates by hand.

Pour into a greased and floured tube pan. Cover lightly with foil but do not seal. Bake at 250 to 275 degrees for 1 1/2 hours or until the cake tests done.

Let cool. Pierce the cake several times with an ice pick. Pour the liqueur over the cake.

Be sure to use a tube pan; the dates will stick in a bundt pan.

Yield: 20 to 25 servings

Mexican Fruitcake

2 cups flour
1¾ cups sugar
2 eggs
2 teaspoons baking soda
1 (20-ounce) can crushed pineapple
1 cup chopped pecans
8 ounces cream cheese, softened
½ cup butter or margarine, softened
2 cups confectioners' sugar
2 to 4 tablespoons chopped pecans

Mix the flour, sugar, eggs and baking soda in a large bowl. Add the undrained pineapple and 1 cup pecans. Pour into a nonstick 9x13-inch cake pan.

Bake at 350 degrees for 35 to 40 minutes or until the cake tests done.

Mix the cream cheese and butter in a bowl. Add the confectioners' sugar and mix well. Spread over the hot cake. Sprinkle with 2 to 4 tablespoons pecans.

Yield: 12 servings

Easy Southern Fruitcake

½ cup butter or margarine
1¼ cups packed dark brown sugar
2 eggs
1¼ cups cake flour
1 teaspoon vanilla extract
1 package mixed candied fruit
2 cups (or more) chopped pecans
¾ cup apple cider
¼ cup rum

Cream the butter and brown sugar in a mixer bowl until light and fluffy. Add the eggs, flour and vanilla and mix well. Add the fruit and pecans. Pack into a greased 4x8-inch loaf pan.

Bake at 275 degrees for 1½ hours.

Pierce the top of the loaf several times. Pour a mixture of the apple cider and rum over the fruitcake. Let cool. Will keep for a long time in an airtight container in the refrigerator.

Yield: 10 to 12 servings

From beautiful Florida Field, to the locker rooms, weight and conditioning area, training and physical therapy complex, squad meeting rooms, practice area, dining and living areas, and the coaches' offices, convenience and quality were paramount when the University of Florida made a commitment in the 1980s to put together one of the most impressive athletic facility complexes in the country. Because everything that was built was designed with the student-athlete in mind, Florida's complex not only rates as one of the premier units in the nation, but it also rates among the most efficient and well-conceived in the country as well. All one has to do is listen to Florida student-athletes talk about the facilities to quickly appreciate how highly they are regarded.

Nell's Hawaiian Delight Cake

1 (16-ounce) can crushed pineapple
2 cups flour
2 teaspoons baking powder
1/2 teaspoon baking soda
1/2 teaspoon salt
1/2 cup butter or margarine, softened
1 1/2 cups sugar
2 eggs
Coconut Pecan Icing
Toasted flaked coconut

Drain the pineapple, reserving 1/2 cup of the juice. Mix the flour, baking powder, baking soda and salt together. Cream the butter in a mixer bowl. Add the sugar gradually, beating constantly. Beat in the eggs 1 at a time. Add the flour mixture and reserved pineapple juice alternately, beating well after each addition and beginning and ending with the flour mixture. Stir in the pineapple. Pour into a greased and floured 10-inch bundt pan. Bake at 350 degrees for 50 to 55 minutes or until the cake tests done. Cool in the pan for 10 minutes. Remove to a plate. Spoon Coconut Pecan Icing over the cake. Let cool. Sprinkle with toasted coconut. Garnish with pineapple slices and leaves.

Yield: 16 servings

Coconut Pecan Icing

1/4 cup butter or margarine, softened
1/2 cup sugar
1/3 cup evaporated milk
1/2 cup flaked coconut
1/2 cup chopped pecans
1/2 teaspoon vanilla extract

Combine the butter, sugar, evaporated milk, coconut and pecans in a small saucepan. Stir in the vanilla. Bring to a boil. Simmer for 3 minutes.

Lemon Poppy Seed Cake

    1 (2-layer) package fat-free or low-fat yellow cake mix
    1/2 cup sugar
    1/3 cup vegetable oil
    1/4 cup water
    1 cup nonfat plain, vanilla or peach yogurt
    1 cup egg substitute
    3 tablespoons lemon juice
    2 tablespoons poppy seeds
    Lemon Glaze (optional)

Combine the cake mix and sugar in a mixer bowl. Add the oil, water, yogurt, egg substitute and lemon juice. Beat at medium speed for 4 minutes. Stir in the poppy seeds. Pour into a 10-cup bundt pan sprayed with nonstick cooking spray. Bake at 350 degrees for 40 minutes or until a wooden pick inserted near the center comes out clean. Cool in the pan on a wire rack for 10 minutes. Remove from the pan. Drizzle with Lemon Glaze. Cool completely on a wire rack.

Yield: 16 servings

Lemon Glaze

    1/2 cup sifted confectioners' sugar
    1 tablespoon lemon juice

Combine the confectioners' sugar and lemon juice in a bowl, stirring until smooth.

Brad's Easy Orange Cake

This recipe was submitted by Monica Culpepper, wife of Brad Culpepper.

1 (2-layer) package butter-recipe yellow cake mix
1 package vanilla instant pudding mix
4 eggs
1/2 cup vegetable oil
1 can mandarin oranges

Combine the cake mix, pudding mix, eggs, oil and undrained oranges in a large mixer bowl and beat well. Pour into a nonstick bundt pan.

Bake at 350 degrees for 40 minutes. Let cool for 10 minutes before serving.

Yield: **10 servings**

Brad Culpepper, the student body vice president, became the nation's premier student-athlete in 1991-92, as he was named the National Toyota/ESPN Leader of the Year for outstanding leadership skills on the field, in the classroom, and in the community; received the National Football Foundation and College Football Hall of Fame Vincent dePaul Draddy scholarship, which honors the nation's outstanding scholar-athlete; was named a first-team GTE Academic All-America; was named to the CFA Scholar-Athlete Team; and was selected for the SEC's Academic Honor Roll for the fourth consecutive year. He now plays for the Tampa Bay Buccaneers.

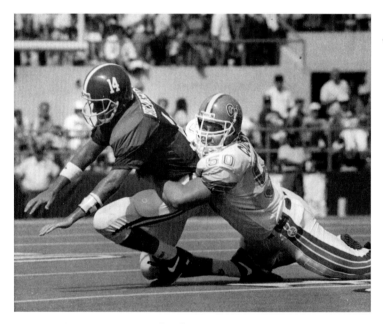

Brad Culpepper in action

Gator Orange Cake

2$\frac{1}{2}$ cups self-rising flour
1$\frac{1}{2}$ cups sugar
$\frac{1}{2}$ cup shortening
3 eggs
1 cup milk
1 teaspoon vanilla extract
3 oranges
2 cups sugar

Sift the flour and 1$\frac{1}{2}$ cups sugar together. Cream the shortening in a mixer bowl until light and fluffy. Add the flour mixture. Add the eggs and $\frac{1}{4}$ cup of the milk.

Beat for 1 minute. Add the remaining $\frac{3}{4}$ cup milk and vanilla. Beat for 2 minutes. Pour into 2 greased and floured 8- or 9-inch round cake pans.

Bake at 325 degrees for 1 hour or until the cake tests done.

Juice the oranges, reserving 1 cup juice. Grate the orange peel. Remove and discard the seeds and pulp. Combine the orange peel, 2 cups sugar and reserved juice in a saucepan. Cook until the mixture forms a light syrup. Spoon the syrup over the cake layers.

Both the cake and icing freeze well separately.

Yield: 12 servings

Grandma Henley's Pound Cake

1¹/₂ cups flour
1 teaspoon baking powder
¹/₈ teaspoon salt
¹/₈ teaspoon mace or vanilla powder
1 cup butter, softened
5 eggs
1¹/₂ cups sugar

Sift the flour, baking powder, salt and mace together. Cream the butter in a large mixer bowl until light and fluffy. Add the flour mixture gradually, beating well after each addition.

Beat the eggs in a medium mixer bowl. Add the sugar and beat until thick. Add the egg mixture to the creamed mixture and beat until very light. Pour into a greased loaf pan or tube pan.

Bake at 300 degrees for 1¹/₂ hours.

Cut into 1-inch slices.

Yield: 15 servings

Praline Cake

1 (2-layer) package yellow cake mix
1 (1-pound) package light brown sugar
2 tablespoons flour
2 eggs, beaten
1 teaspoon vanilla extract
1/2 cup butter
1 1/2 cups chopped pecans

Prepare and bake the cake mix using the package directions for a 9x13-inch cake pan. Mix the brown sugar, flour, eggs and vanilla in a bowl. Melt the butter in a skillet. Add the brown sugar mixture. Stir in the pecans. Spread over the cake.

Bake at 400 degrees for 8 minutes.

Yield: 15 servings

The University of Florida is one of the few schools in the nation that ranks among the elite in both academic and athletic achievement. A lot of schools talk about academic and athletic excellence; upon closer examination, however, there are just a handful of schools in the entire nation that rank among the elite for successful attainment and achievement in both academics and athletics. Count the University of Florida among that elite group.

Prune Cake

2 cups self-rising flour
1³/₄ cups sugar
1 teaspoon cinnamon
1 teaspoon ground cloves
1 teaspoon nutmeg
³/₄ cup vegetable oil
3 eggs
1 small jar baby food prunes
1 cup chopped pecans or walnuts

Combine the flour, sugar, cinnamon, cloves and nutmeg in a large bowl and mix lightly. Mix the oil, eggs and prunes in a small bowl. Add to the flour mixture and mix well. Add the pecans and mix lightly. Pour into a greased and floured tube pan.

Bake at 350 degrees for 1 hour and 10 minutes to 1 hour and 20 minutes.

Yield: 16 servings

Easy Rum Cake

4 eggs
3/4 cup vegetable oil
1 (2-layer) package yellow cake mix
3/4 cup apricot, peach or pear nectar
Rum extract to taste
1 1/4 cups butter
3/4 cup sugar
1/2 cup rum

Combine the eggs, oil, cake mix, apricot nectar and rum extract in a mixer bowl. Beat at medium speed for 5 minutes. Pour into a greased and floured tube pan or bundt pan.

Bake at 350 degrees for 45 minutes or until the cake tests done.

Combine the butter and sugar in a saucepan. Cook until syrupy. Stir in the rum just before the end of the cake baking time. Pour the syrup over the hot cake.

Cool in the pan for 1 hour. Cover the cake with plastic wrap immediately to retain moisture.

Yield: 16 servings

Chompin' Gator Sour Cream Cake

1 cup butter, softened
3 cups sugar
5 large eggs
1 cup sour cream
3 cups cake flour
1/4 teaspoon salt
1/4 teaspoon baking soda
1 teaspoon vanilla extract

Cream the butter and sugar in a mixer bowl until light and fluffy. Add the eggs and beat until the mixture resembles ice cream. Add the sour cream and 1 1/2 cups of the cake flour and mix well. Add the remaining 1 1/2 cups cake flour. Beat for 10 minutes.

Add the salt, baking soda and vanilla and mix well. Pour into a parchment-lined bundt pan. Place the pan in a cold oven. Set the oven temperature to 275 degrees.

Bake for 2 hours.

Cool in the pan on a wire rack for 10 minutes. Remove from the pan to cool completely.

Yield: 16 servings

Strawberry Kiwi Pound Cake

1 (2-layer) package yellow cake mix
4 eggs
3/4 cup vegetable oil
1 (3-ounce) package strawberry-kiwi gelatin
1½ tablespoons hot water
1 small can frozen pink lemonade concentrate
3/4 cup sugar

Combine the cake mix, eggs and oil in a mixer bowl. Beat for 4 minutes. Mix the gelatin with the hot water in a bowl, stirring until cool. Add to the cake mix mixture. Pour into a greased and floured bundt pan.

Bake at 350 degrees for 45 minutes.

Combine the lemonade concentrate and sugar in a blender container. Process until mixed. Pierce the cake several times. Pour the lemonade mixture over the hot cake.

Cool in the pan for several minutes. Invert onto a serving plate.

Yield: 16 servings

Blueberry Pie

1 unbaked pie shell
4 cups blueberries
1 cup sugar
3 tablespoons cornstarch
$1/2$ teaspoon salt
$3/4$ teaspoon grated orange peel
$1/4$ cup water
$1/8$ teaspoon nutmeg
2 tablespoons butter or margarine
Whipped topping

Bake the pie shell at 350 degrees until brown. Pour half the blueberries into the cooled pie crust.

Combine the remaining blueberries, sugar, cornstarch, salt, orange peel, water, nutmeg and butter in a saucepan. Cook until thickened. Pour the filling over the blueberries in the crust.

Chill until serving time. Top with whipped topping.

Yield: 8 servings

Cocoa Pie

1/2 cup baking cocoa
1 1/2 cups sugar
1/4 cup flour or cornstarch
3/4 teaspoon salt
2 cups milk
3 egg yolks
2 teaspoons vanilla extract
1 baked pie shell
3 egg whites
6 tablespoons sugar

Sift the baking cocoa, 1 1/2 cups sugar, flour and salt together. Beat the milk and egg yolks in a bowl. Add the flour mixture and mix well.

Cook in a double boiler until thickened, stirring constantly. Remove from the heat and add the vanilla. Pour into the pie crust.

Beat the egg whites in a mixer bowl until soft peaks form. Add 6 tablespoons sugar gradually, beating constantly until stiff peaks form. Spread the meringue over the pie.

Bake at 350 degrees until the meringue is brown.

Yield: 6 to 8 servings

French Coconut Pies

1 cup butter
1 cup sugar
1 cup light corn syrup
4 eggs
2 unbaked (9-inch) pie shells
2 small cans shredded coconut

Melt the butter in a saucepan. Add the sugar and corn syrup and mix well. Let cool. Beat in the eggs 1 at a time. Pour into the pie shells. Sprinkle with the coconut.

Place the pies in a 475-degree oven. Reduce the oven temperature to 350 degrees. Bake for 45 minutes or until a knife inserted near the center comes out clean.

May cover the pies with foil halfway through the baking time if they begin to brown too much.

Yield: 6 to 8 servings

Egg Custard Pie

4 eggs
$\frac{1}{2}$ cup sugar
$\frac{1}{2}$ teaspoon salt
2 cups half-and-half, scalded
$\frac{1}{2}$ teaspoon vanilla extract
$\frac{1}{8}$ teaspoon almond extract
1 unbaked (9-inch) pie shell
Cinnamon or nutmeg to taste

Beat the eggs lightly in a bowl. Add the sugar and salt. Add the half-and-half and flavorings. Pour into the pie shell. Sprinkle with cinnamon. Bake at 350 degrees for 25 to 30 minutes or until a knife inserted near the center comes out clean.

Yield: 8 servings

Instant Fruit Pie

1 large can crushed pineapple or mixed fruit
1 large package vanilla instant pudding mix
1 cup sour cream
1 graham cracker pie shell
Whipped topping

Mix the pineapple, pudding mix and sour cream in a bowl. Pour into the pie shell. Top with whipped topping. Chill for several hours.

Yield: 6 to 8 servings

Pecan Pie

3 eggs
3/4 cup sugar
3/4 cup corn syrup
1/2 teaspoon salt
1 teaspoon vanilla extract
1 cup pecan halves
3 tablespoons butter, chopped
1 unbaked pie shell

Beat the eggs lightly in a bowl. Add the sugar, syrup, salt, vanilla, pecans and butter and mix well. Pour into the pie shell. Bake at 325 degrees for 50 minutes.

Yield: 6 to 8 servings

Bourbon Pecan Pie

1/2 cup melted butter
1 cup sugar
1 cup light corn syrup
4 eggs, beaten
2 tablespoons bourbon
1/2 cup chocolate chips
1 cup chopped pecans
1 unbaked (9-inch) deep-dish pie shell

Combine the butter, sugar, corn syrup, eggs, bourbon, chocolate chips and pecans in a bowl and mix well. Pour into the pie shell. Bake at 350 degrees for 40 to 45 minutes or until a knife inserted near the center comes out clean; do not overbake. Serve warm with whipped cream or ice cream.

Yield: 8 servings

Strawberry Pies

2 unbaked (9-inch) pie shells
1½ cups sugar
¼ cup cornstarch
⅛ teaspoon salt
1½ cups water
1 large package strawberry gelatin
1½ quarts strawberries

Bake the pie shells at 350 degrees for 15 to 20 minutes or until brown.

Combine the sugar, cornstarch and salt in a saucepan. Add the water. Bring to a rolling boil. Remove from the heat. Add the gelatin and mix well. Combine the cooked mixture and the strawberries in a large bowl and mix well. Pour into the pie crusts. Chill until firm. Serve with whipped cream.

Yield: 8 servings

Trophy Pies

1/2 cup butter
1 (12-ounce) package flaked coconut
1 cup chopped pecans
16 ounces cream cheese, softened
1 can sweetened condensed milk
1 small package whipped topping
2 graham cracker pie shells
1 small jar caramel topping

Melt the butter in a saucepan. Add the coconut and pecans. Cook until the coconut is light brown, stirring frequently. Combine the cream cheese and condensed milk in a mixer bowl. Beat until light and fluffy. Fold in the whipped topping.

Layer half the cream cheese mixture and half the coconut mixture in the pie shells. Swirl half the caramel topping on top. Repeat with the remaining ingredients.

Freeze overnight. Serve frozen or thawed.

Yield: 24 servings

Microwave Apple Crisp

This recipe was contributed by former assistant Lady Gator swimming coach Kim Tesch-Vaught. She swam collegiately for Northwestern University.

1 small package raisins
1 Granny Smith apple, cut into small chunks
1 envelope flavored instant oats
1 tablespoon butter
1 scoop ice cream (optional)

Sprinkle the raisins with a small amount of water. Combine with the apple in a microwave-safe bowl. Sprinkle the oats over the apple mixture. Slice the butter over the mixture.

Microwave for 2 to 3 minutes or until the mixture is heated through and the butter is melted. Toss lightly.

Top with the ice cream. May top with shredded Cheddar cheese instead of ice cream.

Yield: 1 serving

Apple Dumplings

This recipe was contributed by Wanda Aldy, wife of Ron Aldy, former women's associate basketball coach.

> 2 (10-count) cans butter-me-not biscuits
> 1½ to 2½ cups sliced peeled apples
> 2 cups sugar
> 2 cups water
> ½ cup margarine
> Cinnamon to taste
> Vanilla ice cream

Separate and roll out the biscuits. Place the apples on each biscuit, dividing equally. Press the edges together to seal, enclosing the apples. Place in a 9x13-inch glass baking dish.

Bring the sugar, water, margarine and cinnamon to a boil in a saucepan. Pour over the biscuits.

Bake at 325 degrees for 20 to 25 minutes or until brown, spooning the cooking liquid over the biscuits several times.

Top with ice cream.

Yield: 20 servings

Bananas Foster

1/4 cup packed brown sugar
2 tablespoons butter
2 bananas, sliced lengthwise
1/8 teaspoon cinnamon
1 ounce banana liqueur
2 ounces light rum
2 scoops vanilla frozen yogurt

Heat the brown sugar and butter in a chafing dish until the butter melts and the brown sugar dissolves. Add the bananas. Sprinkle with cinnamon.

Pour the liqueur and rum over the top. Ignite carefully. Baste carefully with the warm liquid until the flames die out. Serve immediately over the yogurt.

Yield: 2 servings

Blueberry Crunch

1 large can crushed pineapple
3 cups blueberries
¾ cup sugar
1 (2-layer) package yellow or white cake mix
½ cup melted butter
1 cup chopped pecans or walnuts
¼ cup sugar

Pour the undrained pineapple into a greased 9x12-inch baking dish. Add the blueberries. Sprinkle with ¾ cup sugar. Spread the cake mix over the top.

Drizzle the melted butter over the cake mix. Sprinkle with the pecans and ¼ cup sugar.

Bake at 350 degrees for 35 to 45 minutes or until set. Cut slits in the top approximately halfway through the baking time to allow the juices to escape.

Let stand for 30 minutes or longer before serving.

Yield: 12 to 15 servings

Easy Blueberry Delight

$^1/_4$ cup margarine, softened
3 cups fresh blueberries
$^3/_4$ cup sugar
2 tablespoons flour
2 tablespoons cinnamon
2 tablespoons lemon juice
$^2/_3$ cup milk
$^1/_2$ cup sugar
1 cup flour
1 teaspoon baking powder
$^1/_4$ cup margarine, softened
1 teaspoon vanilla extract
$^3/_4$ cup chopped pecans or walnuts

Spread $^1/_4$ cup margarine in a 9x9-inch baking pan. Combine the blueberries, $^3/_4$ cup sugar, 2 tablespoons flour, cinnamon and lemon juice in a bowl and mix well. Pour into the pan.

Combine the milk, $^1/_2$ cup sugar, 1 cup flour, baking powder, $^1/_4$ cup margarine and vanilla in a mixer bowl and beat until smooth. Drop the batter evenly over the blueberry mixture; the batter will spread during baking. Sprinkle with the pecans.

Bake at 375 degrees for 30 to 45 minutes or until the blueberry mixture is bubbly and the topping is golden brown.

Yield: 6 to 8 servings

Blueberry Cheesecake

1 package graham crackers, crushed
1 cup sugar
1/2 cup butter, softened
2 eggs
1/2 cup sugar
36 ounces cream cheese, softened
2 cans blueberry pie filling
12 ounces whipped topping

Mix the graham cracker crumbs, 1 cup sugar and butter in a bowl. Press into a 9x13-inch baking pan. Beat the eggs with 1/2 cup sugar in a mixer bowl. Add the cream cheese and beat until smooth. Spread over the graham cracker mixture.

Bake at 325 degrees for 20 minutes. Let cool.

Pour the pie filling over the cream cheese mixture. Chill until set. Spread evenly with whipped topping.

Yield: 15 servings

Miniature Cheesecakes

8 ounces cream cheese, softened
1 (14-ounce) can sweetened condensed milk
1/2 cup lemon juice concentrate
1 teaspoon vanilla extract
2 packages miniature phyllo dough shells
1 (21-ounce) can cherry pie filling

Combine the cream cheese, condensed milk, lemon juice and vanilla in a blender container or large mixer bowl. Process or beat until smooth. Spoon into the dough shells. Chill until set. Top with the pie filling before serving.

Yield: 18 servings

Gudula Staub, Florida volleyball

Fruit Cobbler

½ cup melted butter or margarine
1 cup milk
1 cup self-rising flour or baking mix
1 cup sugar
1 teaspoon baking powder (optional)
⅛ teaspoon salt
1 pint any fresh or frozen fruit, such as blackberries, blueberries
 or strawberries; 6 peaches, sliced; 4 apples, sliced; or
 1 (16-ounce) can fruit

Pour the butter into a deep baking pan or ovenproof bowl. Combine the milk, flour, sugar, baking powder and salt in a bowl and mix well. Pour over the butter. Add the fruit. Do not mix.

Bake at 350 degrees for 1 hour.

Serve with ice cream or whipped topping.

Yield: 4 to 6 servings

Caramel Layer Squares

This recipe was contributed by Carol Stoops, wife of defensive coordinator Bob Stoops and mother of Mackenzie.

> 1 (14-ounce) package light caramels
> 1/3 cup evaporated milk
> 1 (2-layer) package pudding-recipe German chocolate cake mix
> 3/4 cup melted butter or margarine
> 1/3 cup evaporated milk
> 1 cup semisweet chocolate chips

Combine the caramels and 1/3 cup evaporated milk in a heavy saucepan. Cook over low heat until the caramels are melted, stirring constantly. Keep warm.

Combine the cake mix, butter and 1/3 cup evaporated milk in a large bowl. Mix until a soft dough forms. Press half the dough into a greased 9x13-inch baking pan.

Bake at 350 degrees for 10 minutes.

Sprinkle the chocolate chips over the crust. Spread with the caramel mixture. Crumble the reserved dough over the top.

Bake for 25 to 30 minutes or until the topping is brown.

Yield: **36 servings**

Chocolate Delight

This recipe was contributed by Regina Stephens, wife of offensive line coach Jimmy Ray Stephens and mother of Chris and Timmy.

½ cup margarine, softened
1 cup flour
1 cup finely chopped pecans
8 ounces cream cheese, softened
1 cup confectioners' sugar
16 ounces whipped topping
3 small packages chocolate instant pudding mix
3 cups milk

Mix the margarine, flour and pecans in a bowl. Press into a 9x13-inch baking pan.

Bake at 350 degrees for 15 minutes. Let cool.

Blend the cream cheese, confectioners' sugar and 1 cup of the whipped topping in a bowl. Spread over the crust. Blend the pudding mix with 3 cups milk in a bowl. Spread over the cream cheese layer. Spread the remaining whipped topping over the top. Chill for several hours.

Yield: 15 servings

Chocolate Candy Bar Dessert

2 cups chocolate graham cracker crumbs
$1/2$ cup melted butter
$1/4$ cup sugar
8 ounces cream cheese, softened
16 ounces whipped topping
$1/4$ cup sugar
8 fun-size candy bars, such as Snickers, Butterfingers or
    Sweet Escapes
1 package chocolate instant pudding mix
1 package vanilla instant pudding mix
3 cups milk

Mix the graham cracker crumbs, butter and $1/4$ cup sugar in a bowl. Pat into a 9x13-inch pan. Chill until needed.

Blend the cream cheese, 1 cup of the whipped topping and $1/4$ cup sugar in a bowl. Spread over the crumb mixture. Crush the candy bars. Sprinkle most of the candy crumbs over the cream cheese layer.

Blend the pudding mixes and milk in a bowl. Pour over the candy crumbs. Top with the remaining whipped topping. Sprinkle with the reserved candy crumbs. Chill for 2 hours.

Yield: 12 servings

Chocolate Gator Crunch

    1 package brownie mix
    2 packages chocolate mousse pie filling mix
    8 ounces whipped topping
    8 Heath bars, crushed
    1 package pecan pieces

Prepare and bake the brownies using the package directions. Let cool. Crumble the brownies. Prepare the mousse using the package directions; reserve the crust for another use. Layer the brownie crumbs, mousse, whipped topping, candy and pecans $1/2$ at a time in a trifle bowl. Chill overnight.

Yield: 8 to 10 servings

Gator Chocolate Mousse

8 ounces semisweet chocolate, chopped into small pieces
8 egg yolks
1 cup sugar
8 egg whites, stiffly beaten
Whipped cream

Heat the chocolate in a double boiler until melted and thick. Turn off the heat. Combine the egg yolks and sugar in a bowl, stirring with a wooden spoon until the mixture is creamy and forms bubbles.

Add the warm chocolate gradually to the egg mixture, stirring constantly. Fold in the egg whites. Pour into tiny cups. Chill for 10 hours or longer. Serve with whipped cream.

Yield: 8 servings

Coach Spurrier's Favorite Dessert

This recipe was contributed by Jerri Spurrier, wife of head football coach Steve Spurrier and mother of Steve, Jr., Lisa, Amy, and Scotty. A native of Ft. Lauderdale, she is a 1967 UF alumna. She is very active in the community and teaches aerobics.

Fresh strawberries
Strawberry glaze
1 angel food cake, cut into halves horizontally
Whipped topping or whipped cream

Slice some of the strawberries; leave the others whole. Combine all the strawberries with the strawberry glaze in a bowl. Spread half the strawberry mixture between the angel food cake layers. Spread the whipped topping over the top and side of the dessert. Pour the remaining strawberry mixture over the dessert.

Yield: 6 to 8 servings

The Spurrier family

Dairy Delight

1 (10-ounce) package Lorna Doone cookies, crushed
1 cup butter, softened
2 packages vanilla instant pudding mix
2 cups milk
1 quart butter pecan ice cream, softened
16 ounces whipped topping
1 package miniature Heath bars, crushed

Mix the cookie crumbs and butter in a bowl. Pat into a 9x13-inch pan. Beat the pudding mix with the milk in a mixer bowl until thick. Fold into the ice cream.

Pour over the crumb mixture. Chill for 2 hours. Spread with the whipped topping. Sprinkle with the candy. Chill until serving time.

Yield: 15 servings

Socially, our university has a healthy atmosphere where students from many different backgrounds enjoy fellowship together. Whatever a student is looking for in a university or in its location can be found in Gainesville, Florida, rated the nation's most livable city in a 1995 national ranking.

Dump Cake Dessert

1 can cherry pie filling
1 large can crushed pineapple
1 (2-layer) package yellow cake mix
1 cup chopped pecans or walnuts
¾ cup margarine, sliced

Layer the pie filling, undrained pineapple, cake mix, pecans and margarine in the order given in a 9x13-inch baking pan.

Bake at 350 degrees for 1 hour.

Yield: 15 servings

Dennis Mitchell (r) and Tony Jones finish first and second in the 55 meter dash at the 1987 SEC Indoor Championships in Gainesville.

Gator Shooters

1 package orange gelatin
1 cup boiling water
1 cup vodka
1 package blue gelatin
1 cup boiling water
1 cup rum
Whipped cream (optional)

Dissolve the orange gelatin in I cup boiling water in a bowl. Add the vodka and mix well. Pour into 50 miniature plastic cups. Dissolve the blue gelatin in I cup boiling water in a bowl. Add the rum and mix well. Pour into 50 miniature plastic cups. Chill until set. Top with whipped cream.

Yield: 100 servings

Gooey Cake Dessert

1 (2-layer) package butter cake mix
1/2 cup butter
1 egg
8 ounces cream cheese, softened
1 (1-pound) package confectioners' sugar
2 eggs
1 cup chopped pecans

Mix the cake mix, butter and 1 egg in a bowl. Press into a 9x13-inch baking pan. Blend the cream cheese, confectioners' sugar and 2 eggs in a bowl until smooth. Pour over the cake mix mixture. Sprinkle with the pecans.

Bake at 325 degrees for 45 minutes.

Yield: 15 servings

We Are the Boys
from Old Florida

*We are the boys from old
Flor-i-da, F-L-O-R-I-D-A,
—Where the girls are the fair-est,
The boys are the squar-est
Of an-y old state down our way.
—We are all strong for old
Flor-i-da, Down where the old
'Ga-tors play.
—In all kinds of weath-er
We'll all stick to-geth-er For
F-L-O-R-I-D-A.*

Green-with-Envy Torte

1/2 cup butter or margarine
1 cup graham cracker crumbs
1 cup saltine crumbs
2 (3-ounce) packages pistachio instant pudding mix
1 1/2 cups cold milk
1 quart vanilla or butter pecan ice cream, softened
16 ounces whipped topping
3 Heath bars, crushed

Melt the butter in a 9x13-inch baking pan. Sprinkle the cracker crumbs over the butter.

Bake at 350 degrees for 10 minutes. Let cool.

Beat the pudding mix, milk and ice cream in a mixer bowl for 2 minutes. Pour over the crust. Top with the whipped topping. Sprinkle with the candy. Chill until serving time.

Yield: 15 servings

Old-Fashioned Lemon "Cheesecake"

1/2 cup butter, softened
1/4 cup vegetable oil
1 1/2 cups sugar
3 eggs, at room temperature
3/4 cup plus 2 tablespoons milk
2 1/3 cups sifted flour
1 tablespoon baking powder
1/4 teaspoon salt
2 teaspoons lemon extract
1/3 cup cornstarch
1/2 cup cold water
1 1/2 cups sugar
Grated peel of 3 lemons
1 cup lemon juice
2 eggs, beaten
1 cup hot water
1/4 teaspoon salt

Cream the butter, oil and 1 1/2 cups sugar in a mixer bowl. Add 3 eggs and beat well. Add the milk, flour, baking powder and 1/4 teaspoon salt and mix gently without beating. Add the lemon flavoring.

Pour into 4 greased cake pans with levers for releasing the cake. The layers will be very thin.

Bake at 300 degrees for 7 to 8 minutes; do not brown. Cool slightly. Invert onto a plate; cover with a second plate and invert onto the second plate. Let cool.

Dissolve the cornstarch in the cold water and set aside. Combine 1 1/2 cups sugar, lemon peel, lemon juice, 2 eggs and hot water in a saucepan. Add 1/4 teaspoon salt. Cook over low heat until the mixture begins to bubble, stirring constantly. Add the cornstarch mixture, stirring briskly.

Cool in a pan of cold water. Spread between the layers and over the top of the "cheesecake."

Yield: 15 servings

Lush Dessert

1 cup self-rising flour
1/2 cup melted margarine
1/2 cup chopped pecans or walnuts
1 cup confectioners' sugar
8 ounces whipped topping
8 ounces cream cheese, softened
1 tablespoon lemon juice
1 can fruit pie filling
1/2 cup chopped pecans or walnuts

Stir the flour into the margarine in a bowl. Pat into a 9x13-inch baking dish. Sprinkle with 1/2 cup pecans. Press the pecans into the flour mixture.

Bake at 350 degrees for 10 minutes or just until the crust begins to rise in the center. Let cool.

Beat the confectioners' sugar, 1 cup of the whipped topping, cream cheese and lemon juice in a bowl. Spread over the crust. Spread the pie filling over the cream cheese layer. Top with the remaining whipped topping. Sprinkle with 1/2 cup pecans.

Yield: 18 servings

Pavlova

This recipe was contributed by former Lady Gator tennis player Jillian Alexander. She won the 1991 Volvo Doubles of the Year, was named to the 1991 Rolex All-Star Team, and was named All-America in singles and doubles in 1990-1991.

8 egg whites
1/8 teaspoon salt
1 (16-ounce) package superfine sugar
2 teaspoons cornstarch
2 teaspoons white vinegar
1 teaspoon vanilla extract
Whipped cream
Fresh fruit, such as grapes, strawberries, peaches, pears, plums and/or kiwifruit

Cut a 7- to 8-inch circle from foil; place on a baking sheet.

Beat the egg whites with the salt in a mixer bowl until soft peaks form. Add the sugar gradually, beating constantly until stiff peaks form.

Add the cornstarch, vinegar and vanilla and beat for 1 minute. Pile the mixture on the foil, approximately 3 inches high at the sides and lower in the center.

Bake at 300 degrees for 10 minutes. Reduce the oven temperature to 225 degrees. Bake for 1 hour and 20 minutes. Turn off the oven. Let stand with the door ajar until cold.

Fill with whipped cream and fruit.

Yield: 6 to 8 servings

Pear Crisp

6 to 8 large pears, peeled, sliced
1 cup sugar
1 cup flour
1 teaspoon vanilla extract
$^1/_2$ cup margarine or butter

Place the pears in a buttered 9x13-inch baking dish. Combine the sugar, flour and vanilla in a bowl. Cut in the margarine until crumbly. Sprinkle over the pears.

Bake at 350 degrees for 1 to 1$^1/_2$ hours or until the pears are tender.

Do not use Bartlett pears in this recipe.

Yield: 6 servings

Gator cheerleaders reach for victory.

Ribbon Delight

1 (15-ounce) can fruit cocktail
Graham crackers
1/4 cup butter or margarine, softened
1 cup confectioners' sugar
2 tablespoons evaporated milk
1 (3-ounce) package strawberry gelatin
1 cup boiling water
1/2 cup evaporated milk

Drain the fruit cocktail, reserving 1/2 cup of the juice. Line a 6x12-inch glass dish with graham crackers.

Place the butter in a bowl. Add the confectioners' sugar 2 tablespoons at a time, mixing well after each addition. Beat in 2 tablespoons evaporated milk. Spread over the graham crackers in the dish. Top with another layer of graham crackers. Chill until needed.

Dissolve the gelatin in the boiling water in a bowl. Divide into 2 equal parts. Stir 1/2 cup evaporated milk into half the gelatin mixture. Chill until firm. Beat with a fork until fluffy. Pour over the graham cracker layers. Chill until firm.

Stir the reserved fruit cocktail juice into the remaining gelatin mixture. Add the fruit cocktail. Chill until slightly firm. Pour over the dessert, spreading to cover the top. Chill overnight. Cut into 8 squares.

Yield: 8 servings

Strawberry Shortcake

4 to 5 pints fresh strawberries, hulled
1 to 2 cups sugar
2 cups flour
1/2 cup sugar
2 teaspoons baking powder
1/8 teaspoon salt
1 tablespoon butter, softened
1 cup milk
Softened butter

Place the strawberries in a large bowl. Add 1 to 2 cups sugar gradually, chopping with a spoon until the strawberries are very juicy. Set aside.

Mix the flour, 1/2 cup sugar, baking powder, salt, 1 tablespoon butter and milk in a bowl. Pour into a 9x9-inch baking dish or baking pan.

Bake at 350 degrees for 25 minutes or until a wooden pick inserted near the center comes out clean. Let cool.

Cut the shortcake horizontally into 2 layers. Spread 1 layer with butter and cover with strawberries. Top with the remaining layer. Spread with butter. Make several slash marks in the top layer.

Cover with the remaining strawberries, spooning back onto the top any strawberries or juice that falls off.

Yield: 8 servings

Contributors

Missy Aggertt
Wanda Aldy
Jillian Alexander
Vida Alexander
Neal Anderson
Susie Baseheart
Sue Boate
Judy Boles
Paula Bowlan
Mary Jane Braddock
Andy Brandi
Doris Bratcher
Madge Brownlee
Rhea Broyles
Becky Burleigh
Norm Carlson
Marsha Casady
Donna Chapin
Renae Clements
Errophene Crozier
Brad Culpepper
Monica Culpepper
Diane Cutler
Cathy Dickson
Bobbie Dockery
Cheryl Doering
Billy Donovan
Lynn Dowling
Lisa Duncanson
Jane Edmondson
Pat Evans
Gladys Feussner
Betty Fish
Joni Florence
Claire France
Deborah Franks
Pat Frazier
Diane Gebhardt
Sue Goodwin
Opal Graves
Martha Jane Green
Vinell Griggs

Mary Hafeman
Chris Hagin
Alma Haines
Dorothy Harber
Elaine Harden
Millie Harris
Miriam Haywood
Beth Herrington
Irma Henley
Cathy Holland
Nancy Holloway
Lois Houston
Kimberly Humphries
Suellen Johnson
John James
Julie Jones
June Jones
Judy Kensler
Barbara Kingry
Monika Kirkpatrick
Ruth Ann Klockowski
Cathy Knight
Suanne Knopf
Joyce Laboy
Mary Beth Lassiter
Shirley Laxton
Cathryn Lombardi
Amy MacLean
Susan MacLean
Dolores Manning
Judi Markell
Nita Mata
Mary Helen McCallum
Mary McCloskey
Jean Meisner
Dottie Moore
Rhoda Jean Moore
Nancy Moss
Lavelle Mount
Faye Mullinax
Linda Newman
Muriel Osburn

Joann Page
Tere Page
Betty Parrish
Charley Pell
Ward Pell
Wendy Person
Anne Perusek
Nancy Price
Kathy Putnam
Sue Rappenecker
Bobby Raymond
Debbie Rhodes
Storm Roberts
Dawn Robinette
Ann Marie Rogers
Rhonda Rogers
Linda Roszel
JoAnn Rowell
Thelma Saltsman
Laraine Sapp
Renee Servatt
Beverly "Jake" Smith
Frances Smith
Becky Spence
Bonita Spidell
Jerri Spurrier
Cecelia Staley
Regina Stephens
Carol Stoops
Paula Strawn
Carolyn Surrency
Kim Tesch-Vaught
Kevin Thornton
Delores Tumbleson
Quenta Vettel
Diana Vogel
Yvonne Waters
Chris Weaver
Les Wells
Libby Williams
Jean Wilson
Katie Yeckring

Index

Complete the Order Form, include your check or credit card information and mail to:

**GATOR
*Championship Recipes***
P.O. Box 12958
Gainesville, FL 32604
FAX Order to: (352) 591–0751

Checks payable to:
**GATOR
*Championship Recipes***

Method of Payment
☐ MasterCard ☐ Visa
☐ Check or Money Order

Card Number _____

Exp. Date _____

Please Print
(Please type or use dark ink)

Name _____

Address _____

City _____ State ____ Zip ____

Home Phone ( )_____

Day Phone ( )_____

QTY	DESCRIPTION	UNIT PRICE	AMOUNT
	GATOR *Championship Recipes*	$19.96	
	Orders Will Be Shipped After October 1, 1997	FL Residents add 6% Sales Tax	
		Postage & Handling	$5.00/per book
		TOTAL	

Signature _____

Complete the Order Form, include your check or credit card information and mail to:

**GATOR
*Championship Recipes***
P.O. Box 12958
Gainesville, FL 32604
FAX Order to: (352) 591–0751

Checks payable to:
**GATOR
*Championship Recipes***

Method of Payment
☐ MasterCard ☐ Visa
☐ Check or Money Order

Card Number _____

Exp. Date _____

Please Print
(Please type or use dark ink)

Name _____

Address _____

City _____ State ____ Zip ____

Home Phone ( )_____

Day Phone ( )_____

QTY	DESCRIPTION	UNIT PRICE	AMOUNT
	GATOR *Championship Recipes*	$19.96	
	Orders Will Be Shipped After October 1, 1997	FL Residents add 6% Sales Tax	
		Postage & Handling	$5.00/per book
		TOTAL	

Signature _____

Complete the Order Form, include your check or credit card information and mail to:

GATOR
Championship Recipes
P.O. Box 12958
Gainesville, FL 32604
FAX Order to: (352) 591–0751

Checks payable to:
GATOR
Championship Recipes

Method of Payment
☐ MasterCard ☐ Visa
☐ Check or Money Order

Card Number _____

Exp. Date _____

Please Print
(Please type or use dark ink)

Name _____

Address _____

City _____ State _____ Zip _____

Home Phone ( ) _____

Day Phone ( ) _____

QTY	DESCRIPTION	UNIT PRICE	AMOUNT
	GATOR *Championship Recipes*	$19.96	
	Orders Will Be Shipped After October 1, 1997	FL Residents add 6% Sales Tax	
		Postage & Handling	$5.00/per book
		TOTAL	

Signature _____

Complete the Order Form, include your check or credit card information and mail to:

GATOR
Championship Recipes
P.O. Box 12958
Gainesville, FL 32604
FAX Order to: (352) 591–0751

Checks payable to:
GATOR
Championship Recipes

Method of Payment
☐ MasterCard ☐ Visa
☐ Check or Money Order

Card Number _____

Exp. Date _____

Please Print
(Please type or use dark ink)

Name _____

Address _____

City _____ State _____ Zip _____

Home Phone ( ) _____

Day Phone ( ) _____

QTY	DESCRIPTION	UNIT PRICE	AMOUNT
	GATOR *Championship Recipes*	$19.96	
	Orders Will Be Shipped After October 1, 1997	FL Residents add 6% Sales Tax	
		Postage & Handling	$5.00/per book
		TOTAL	

Signature _____